Wellness Over Fortune: Investing in Heath Pays The Best Dividends

MORGAN HARTWELL

Published by Richard Bakyeayiri, 2024.

While every precaution has been taken in the preparation of this book, the publisher assumes no responsibility for errors or omissions, or for damages resulting from the use of the information contained herein.

WELLNESS OVER FORTUNE: INVESTING IN HEATH PAYS THE BEST DIVIDENDS

First edition. November 19, 2024.

Copyright © 2024 MORGAN HARTWELL.

ISBN: 979-8227844354

Written by MORGAN HARTWELL.

Also by MORGAN HARTWELL

Wellness Over Fortune: Investing in Heath Pays The Best Dividends

Table of Contents

Wellness Over Fortune: Investing in Heath Pays The Best Dividends.........1
INTRODUCTION..2
CHAPTER 1..4
CHAPTER 2..12
CHAPTER 3..21
CHAPTER 4..34
CHAPTER 5..46
CHAPTER 6..59

INTRODUCTION

In today's fast-paced world, where success is often synonymous with financial wealth and material possessions, the true essence of prosperity often gets overshadowed. "Wellness Over Fortune: Investing in Health Pays the Best Dividends" is not just a title; it's a mantra for a fulfilling and thriving life. In this transformative narrative, we delve into the profound connection between well-being and wealth, uncovering the hidden treasures that lie in prioritizing health.

Picture this: a bustling cityscape filled with individuals chasing after elusive fortunes, sacrificing their health at the altar of success. But what if I told you that the key to lasting prosperity isn't found in the size of your bank account, but in the state of your well-being? This paradigm shift is where "Wellness Over Fortune" takes center stage, challenging conventional wisdom and offering a fresh perspective on what it truly means to invest in yourself.

As we embark on this journey of self-discovery and enlightenment, it becomes clear that our most valuable asset is not our financial portfolio, but our physical, mental, and emotional health. The concept of investing in health as a means of reaping the most rewarding dividends is a revolutionary idea that transcends traditional notions of wealth.

In a society where incessant hustling and persistent pursuit of achievement can lead to burnout and tiredness, "Wellness Over Fortune" acts as a guiding light, illuminating the route to a more balanced and satisfying life. Through stories of resilience, transforming experiences, and evidence-based techniques, this book brings to the forefront the need of prioritizing self-care and well-being in a world that emphasizes activity and achievement.

But this isn't just another self-help book promoting vague promises of instant gratification. "Wellness Over Fortune" is a philosophy for sustainable living, where every decision, from the food we consume to the activities we engage in, is a conscious choice towards a healthier and happier future. It's a call to action for individuals to reclaim their power and prioritize their well-being above all else.

At its core, this book is a celebration of the human spirit and its capacity for growth, resilience, and renewal. It's a reminder that genuine riches is not measured in tangible belongings, but in the vitality and vigor with which we approach life. By embracing the philosophy of "Wellness Over Fortune," we unlock the door to a world of abundance, where health is the ultimate currency and well-being is the foundation upon which all other achievements are built.

So, my reader, are you ready to start on a voyage of self-discovery and transformation? Are you willing to disrupt the existing quo and alter your concept of success? If so, join me as we explore the deep reality that investing in health offers the finest benefits, leading to a life filled with vitality, purpose, and true success. Welcome to "Wellness Over Fortune," where the riches of well-being await those daring enough to seek them.

CHAPTER 1
The Foundations of Health

Health is the cornerstone of a meaningful and vigorous life, weaving together the intricate threads of physical, mental, and emotional well-being to create a tapestry of vitality and strength. The cultivation of holistic wellness that supports all facets of our being is the foundation of health, rather than just the absence of disease. As we continue on a quest to find the pillars that uphold our health, let us study the interwoven aspects that create the foundations of well-being.

At the core of our health foundation lies nutrition, the food that feeds our bodies and minds, giving the building blocks for development and repair. Consuming a diet that is well-balanced and full of whole foods, fruits, vegetables, lean meats, and healthy fats is similar to taking care of a garden in that it gives our bodies the critical ingredients they require to flourish. With each bite, we have the potential to support our immune system, improve our energy levels, and defend against chronic diseases, creating a firm footing for long-term health and vitality.

Alongside nutrition stands physical exercise, the dynamic energy that breaths life into our bodies, revitalizing our muscles, bones, and organs with the rhythm of movement. Exercise is the symphony that harmonizes our physical and emotional well-being. It can take many forms, from gentle walks in the outdoors to intense yoga sessions and heart-pounding aerobic exercises. Through regular activity, we strengthen our cardiovascular system, improve our flexibility and balance, and enhance our mood and cognitive function, establishing a firm foundation of health that radiates throughout our entire being.

An additional pillar of our health foundation is mental and emotional well-being, which shapes our inner world and impacts our experiences outside of it. Our mental resilience is nourished by engaging in self-care routines, mindfulness, and meditation. These practices help us maintain emotional equilibrium, clarity, and focus when facing life's obstacles. We strengthen the foundation of our mental health by developing a strong sense of self-awareness and compassion, which fortifies it and provides a safe haven from potential anxiety, stress, and uncertainty storms.

Sleep, often touted as the unsung hero of health, plays a key role in setting the framework for overall well-being. Our bodies respond rejuvenatingly to rest and excellent sleep, which facilitates hormone balance, memory consolidation, and cellular repair. Respecting our bodies' innate sleep cycles and establishing a sleep-friendly atmosphere helps us maintain a fundamental aspect of health that underpins our mental clarity, emotional stability, and physical vigor.

Establishing and maintaining social ties and participating in the community are essential elements of our health base, providing us with a feeling of purpose, support, and community. Our emotional health and mental toughness are influenced by developing deep connections, encouraging empathy, and taking part in enjoyable social activities. We fortify the foundation of our health via genuine connections, mutual support, and shared experiences, building a network of support that helps us both in difficult and happy times.

Self-care routines, practices, and habits are the gentle hands that tend to our wellbeing, cultivating a culture of self-compassion and love that is the cornerstone of our overall health. Self-care rituals serve as the protectors of our health, maintaining our vigor and radiance in the face of life's obstacles and responsibilities. They can range from daily regimens that emphasize hydration, skincare, and relaxation to times of isolation and introspection that uplift our spirits.

Health is largely shaped by environmental variables as well, including exposure to chemicals, water quality, and air quality. We contribute to the longevity and vitality of our health foundation by establishing a clean, sustainable living environment that promotes our well-being and protects our bodies and brains from potential dangers and contaminants that could jeopardize our general wellness.

It is crucial to keep in mind that our foundation for health is dynamic and ever-changing, requiring constant care, attention, and adaptation in order to flourish as we traverse the challenging landscape of health and well-being. We empower ourselves to prioritize our health and well-being by practicing mindfulness, resilience, and self-awareness. This helps us create a solid foundation that supports us in all facets of our lives.

The foundations of health are essentially a symphony of interwoven components that work in unison to create a vibrant and resilient tapestry of well-being. These components include sleep, social connections, mental and emotional well-being, physical activity, nutrition, and self-care practices. We create the foundation for a life full of vitality, purpose, and long-lasting health that transcends time and circumstance by carefully tending to these fundamental pillars with intention and compassion.

Understanding Holistic Wellness

The multifaceted notion of holistic wellness encompasses the interrelated dynamics of physical, mental, emotional, and spiritual well-being and goes beyond the traditional definition of health. Holistic wellness weaves together the threads of self-care, mindfulness, nutrition, movement, and emotional balance to create a tapestry of resilience and vitality. It is fundamentally a harmonious symphony of mind, body, and spirit. The realization that every person is a complex, interconnected system with physical, mental, emotional, and spiritual dimensions that profoundly influence one another is at the heart of the holistic wellness movement. Holistic wellness is an approach to health that nurtures every aspect of our being and fosters a deep sense of alignment, balance, and harmony within ourselves and with the world around us. Physical well-being is a foundational pillar of holistic wellness, encompassing the care and nourishment of the body through healthy nutrition, regular physical activity, adequate rest, and preventive healthcare practices. Holistic wellness acknowledges the intricate interplay between these dimensions and seeks to cultivate a state of optimal well-being that encompasses all aspects of human experience. In order to support our immune system, metabolism, cardiovascular health, and general longevity, we must honor the body as a sacred vessel that holds our essence and vitality. Mental and emotional well-being are also crucial elements of holistic wellness, as they influence our quality of life, emotional resilience, and cognitive function. Practices such as mindfulness, meditation, therapy, and self-reflection enable us to cultivate a deeper awareness of our thoughts, emotions, and beliefs, fostering mental clarity, emotional balance, and psychological resilience in the face of life's challenges and stressors.

Embracing emotional intelligence and self-awareness allows us to navigate the complexities of our inner landscape with grace and compassion, fostering a sense of inner peace and fulfillment that transcends external circumstances. By acknowledging and honoring our emotions as valuable messengers and guides, we create space for healing, growth, and transformation within ourselves, deepening our capacity for empathy, connection, and authenticity in our relationships with others.

Spiritual well-being, often overlooked in traditional healthcare paradigms, is an integral component of holistic wellness that encompasses our sense of purpose, meaning, and connection to something greater than ourselves. Cultivating a sense of spiritual awareness and connection can provide profound comfort, guidance, and inspiration in navigating life's challenges, uncertainties, and transitions, fostering a deep sense of inner peace, wisdom, and fulfillment.

Holistic wellness also acknowledges the interconnectedness of individuals with their environment, recognizing the impact of our physical surroundings, social relationships, and lifestyle choices on our health and well-being. By fostering a sense of environmental stewardship, social responsibility, and community engagement, we create a supportive and nurturing context that promotes well-being for ourselves, others, and the planet as a whole.

Mindful nutrition, grounded movement practices, restorative sleep, stress management techniques, and creative self-expression are just a few of the tools and pathways through which we can cultivate holistic wellness in our lives. By embracing a holistic approach to health that integrates these dimensions, we empower ourselves to reclaim agency over our well-being and lead lives of meaning, purpose, and vitality.

In essence, understanding holistic wellness is about recognizing the interconnectedness of all aspects of our being—body, mind, emotions, and spirit—and cultivating a state of harmony, balance, and alignment within ourselves and with the world around us. By honoring the complexity and wholeness of our human experience, we can embark on a transformative journey of self-discovery, healing, and growth that transcends the limitations of conventional healthcare paradigms and empowers us to live lives of radiant health, vitality, and well-being.

As we delve deeper into the depths of holistic wellness, we uncover a tapestry of interconnected threads that weave together the rich fabric of our human experience. Each thread—nutrition, movement, mindfulness, emotional balance, spiritual connection, environmental awareness, and social engagement—contributes to the intricate tapestry of holistic wellness, creating a vibrant and resilient foundation upon which we can build a life of profound well-being, purpose, and fulfillment. By embracing the essence of holistic wellness and honoring the interconnectedness of all aspects of our being, we open the door to a transformative journey of self-discovery, healing, and growth that nourishes the body, mind, heart, and spirit in profound and lasting ways.

THE MIND-BODY CONNECTION

The mind-body connection is a profound and intricate relationship that transcends the boundaries of physicality and consciousness, intertwining the realms of thought, emotion, sensation, and physiological response in a seamless dance of interdependence and influence. It is a dynamic synergy that lies at the core of our existence, shaping our perceptions, behaviors, and overall well-being in ways that extend far beyond the limitations of either the mind or the body alone.

At the heart of the mind-body connection is the recognition that our thoughts, beliefs, emotions, and experiences have a profound impact on our physical health, vitality, and resilience. The mind, with its vast reservoir of thoughts, memories, and perceptions, serves as a powerful orchestrator of our physiological responses, influencing everything from our heart rate and immune function to our hormonal balance and cellular health.

When we experience stress, anxiety, or negative emotions, the mind sends signals to the body that trigger the release of stress hormones such as cortisol and adrenaline, initiating a cascade of physiological changes designed to prepare us for fight or flight. While this response is crucial for our survival in acute situations, chronic stress and negative emotions can have detrimental effects on our health and well-being, contributing to a wide range of physical ailments such as heart disease, digestive disorders, immune dysfunction, and chronic pain.

Conversely, positive emotions, thoughts, and beliefs have been shown to have a profound healing effect on the body, promoting relaxation, emotional balance, and overall well-being. The mind-body connection operates in a bidirectional manner, with our physical health and vitality also influencing our mental and emotional states. When we nourish our bodies with wholesome nutrition, regular exercise, restful sleep, and supportive relationships, we create a solid foundation for mental clarity, emotional resilience, and spiritual growth.

The mind-body connection is not merely a theoretical concept but a tangible reality that is supported by a growing body of scientific research and empirical evidence. Studies in the fields of psychoneuroimmunology, neuroplasticity, and mind-body medicine have demonstrated the intricate ways in which our thoughts, emotions, behaviors, and beliefs impact our physical health and well-being, reshaping our neural circuitry, immune function, gene expression, and overall physiology.

Mind-body practices such as mindfulness meditation, yoga, tai chi, and breath work have emerged as powerful tools for cultivating awareness, relaxation, and self-regulation, harnessing the innate healing capacities of the mind-body connection to promote health, resilience, and vitality. By bringing conscious awareness to our thoughts, emotions, and bodily sensations, we can cultivate inner peace, emotional balance, and physical well-being, fostering a sense of wholeness and integration that transcends the limitations of the dualistic mind-body dichotomy.

In exploring the depths of the mind-body connection, we uncover the profound wisdom of the body as a sacred vessel of consciousness, mirroring the intricate tapestry of our innermost thoughts, emotions, and beliefs. The body speaks to us in the language of sensations, symptoms, and signals, serving as a barometer of our inner state and an invaluable guide on our journey of self-discovery and healing.

Embracing the mind-body connection invites us to cultivate a deeper sense of self-awareness, self-acceptance, and self-compassion, honoring the interconnectedness of our thoughts, emotions, and physical sensations as valuable messengers and teachers. By listening to the wisdom of our bodies, we can uncover the root causes of our physical symptoms and emotional patterns, addressing them at their source with mindfulness, compassion, and presence.

The mind-body connection offers us a gateway to holistic healing and transformation, inviting us to explore the depths of our inner landscape with curiosity, courage, and openness. By integrating the wisdom of the mind and the body, we can create a harmonious relationship that fosters health, vitality, and resilience on all levels of our being, cultivating a deep sense of alignment, balance, and integration that supports our journey of self-discovery and growth.

In essence, the mind-body connection is a sacred dance of consciousness and embodiment, inviting us to embrace the full spectrum of our human experience with awareness, presence, and reverence. It is a journey of self-discovery, healing, and transformation that transcends the limitations of the dualistic mind-body paradigm, inviting us to explore the depths of our inner wisdom and navigate the complexities of our physical, mental, emotional, and spiritual dimensions with grace, compassion, and authenticity.

As we deepen our understanding of the mind-body connection, we awaken to the inherent power and potential that resides within us, empowering us to cultivate health, vitality, and well-being from the inside out. By honoring the interdependence and synergy of our thoughts, emotions, and physical sensations, we unlock the key to profound healing, growth, and transformation, reclaiming our innate capacity to thrive and flourish in harmony with the wisdom of the mind-body connection.

CHAPTER 2
Wealth of Health-Investing in Yourself

In the bustling landscape of modern life, amidst the flurry of deadlines, commitments, and distractions that vie for our attention, there is a profound truth that often gets overshadowed by the glamour of success and material wealth – the wealth of health. In a world where productivity and achievement are glorified, the true essence of well-being and self-care can easily be relegated to the sidelines. However, what if we reframed our understanding of wealth, not merely in terms of monetary riches, but as a holistic investment in ourselves, our health, and our overall well-being?

Imagine a scenario where you are presented with two choices – one offering immediate financial gain but at the expense of your health and vitality, and the other requiring you to prioritize self-care, nourishment, and mindfulness, leading to a wealth of health that transcends monetary value. Which path would you choose? In a society driven by the pursuit of external success and validation, it is easy to overlook the intrinsic value of investing in our most precious asset – our health.

True wealth extends far beyond the boundaries of material possessions and monetary wealth; it encompasses the richness of a vibrant, resilient body, a clear, focused mind, and a joyful, balanced spirit. Investing in yourself is not merely a luxury reserved for the privileged few; it is a fundamental necessity that lays the foundation for a life of abundance, purpose, and fulfillment. Just as we allocate resources towards financial investments, career advancement, and external pursuits, so too should we prioritize the investment of time, energy, and intention towards nurturing our physical, mental, and emotional well-being.

The concept of 'Wealth of Health' invites us to adopt a paradigm shift in our approach to self-care and well-being, viewing the cultivation of health as a strategic investment that yields exponential returns in all areas of our lives. When we prioritize our health, we cultivate a sense of vitality, resilience, and inner balance that empowers us to navigate the challenges and uncertainties of life with grace, poise, and confidence. Rather than viewing health as a passive state of absence of illness, we can redefine it as an active pursuit of optimal well-being, vitality, and wholeness.

Investing in yourself goes beyond the realms of physical fitness and nutrition; it encompasses a multifaceted approach to holistic well-being that integrates the dimensions of mind, body, and spirit. Just as a diversified investment portfolio ensures long-term financial stability, so too does a holistic approach to health and wellness safeguard our overall vitality and resilience. By nurturing our physical body through regular exercise, nourishing food, and restful sleep, we lay the groundwork for a strong foundation of health that supports our mental clarity, emotional balance, and spiritual growth.

The adage "health is wealth" holds true in a world where the pace of life is frenetic, the demands are relentless, and the pressure to excel is ever-present. In the pursuit of external success and validation, it is easy to neglect the subtle whispers of our body, mind, and spirit, urging us to slow down, breathe deeply, and reconnect with the essence of our being. Investing in yourself is a radical act of self-love and self-respect that acknowledges the intrinsic value of your health and well-being above all else.

The 'Wealth of Health' paradigm encourages us to shift our focus from external validation and comparison towards a deep, inner knowing of our inherent worth and value. Rather than measuring our success by external metrics such as wealth, status, or achievement, we can gauge our prosperity by the quality of our relationships, the depth of our self-awareness, and the resonance of our inner joy. True wealth rests not in the amassing of material belongings, but in the cultivation of meaningful experiences, emotional connections, and a strong feeling of purpose and fulfillment.

Investing in yourself is a radical act of self-empowerment that transcends societal expectations and norms, honoring the unique journey of self-discovery, growth, and transformation that leads to a life of abundance, authenticity, and alignment. When we invest in our health, we invest in our future, building the framework for a life of vibrancy, meaning, and resilience that extends far beyond the boundaries of external achievement and recognition. The true measure of prosperity resides not in the amassing of external trappings, but in the cultivation of inner riches that nourish the spirit and illuminate the path towards true contentment and well-being.

The 'Wealth of Health' is a powerful reminder of the inherent importance of investing in yourself, your health, and your general well-being as a sacred act of self-love, self-respect, and self-empowerment. By embracing a holistic approach to health and wellness, we may unlock the unlimited potential that lives inside us, fostering a life of plenty, energy, and thriving that surpasses the confines of external achievement and recognition. May this paradigm shift inspire you to prioritize your health, nurture your well-being, and invest in yourself as a path to true wealth and fulfillment on all levels of your being.

Nurturing Physical Well-being

Physical well-being, the cornerstone of a lively and meaningful life, serves as the groundwork upon which our everyday pursuits and aspirations are formed. It covers not only the absence of illness but the active cultivation of power, vitality, and resilience in our bodies. Nurturing physical well-being is a very personal journey that intertwines the realms of movement, nourishment, rest, and self-care to produce a harmonic symphony of health and vigor.

At the heart of cultivating physical well-being lies the art of movement — the dance of muscles, bones, and breath that animates our bodies and invigorates our emotions. Movement is not only a means to an end but a delightful celebration of our physical skills and potential. Whether through the rhythmic hammering of feet on a running course, the smooth flow of a yoga sequence, or the dynamic intensity of a dancing class, movement links us to the inherent strength and agility that live inside us.

When we move our bodies with intention and attention, we awaken latent muscles, increase circulation, and release tension, creating a sensation of aliveness and vigor that permeates every area of our being. The act of movement is a sacred rite that honors the temple of our body, allowing us to express ourselves, connect with our physicality, and tap into the wellspring of energy and resilience that resides at our heart.

When it comes to maintaining our physical health, food is crucial to providing our bodies with the vital nutrients, vitamins, and minerals they require to function at their best. Beyond simple nutrition, nourishment is an embodied practice of awareness, appreciation, and reverence for the life-giving gifts of nature that support our health and vitality. Whether it comes from colorful fruits and veggies, whole grains, lean meats, or refreshing drinks, nourishing oneself on a daily basis is an act of self-love and self-care that respects our bodies' inherent intelligence.

When we fuel ourselves with nutritious, nutrient-dense foods, we supply our bodies with the building blocks needed for maximum health, energy, and vitality. From the vivid hues of a rainbow salad to the comfortable warmth of a nutritious soup, each meal is an opportunity to nurture our bodies, brains, and spirits with the healing power of whole foods that support our well-being and nourish our soul.

After the rigors and stressors of everyday life, rest—the silent partner in the dance of physical well-being—is essential for refueling, revitalizing, and rebuilding our bodies. The art of rest frequently loses out to the unrelenting pursuit of success and achievement on the outside in a society that exalts bustle and productivity. But rather than being a luxury that only the wealthy can afford, sleep is an essential requirement for maintaining our mental, emotional, and physical health.

We make room for rest, recovery, and rejuvenation that refuels our energy reserves and improves our general vitality when we respect our body's innate cycles and signals for relaxation. Sleeping soundly, practicing mindfulness, or engaging in soul-stirring activities are all ways that rest is a sacred invitation to slow down, check in, and re-establish a connection with the body's intrinsic knowledge that directs us toward equilibrium and wellbeing.

Self-care, the gentle skill of tending to our physical, emotional, and spiritual needs with compassion and kindness, is a cornerstone of nurturing physical well-being. Self-care is an intense act of self-love and self-respect that recognizes the inherent worth of our vitality and well-being rather than being a self-indulgent luxury. Self-care is a life-changing activity that promotes a profound sense of connection and harmony with our genuine selves, whether it takes the shape of calming baths, tender massages, or nourishing rituals that replenish our energy.

We build a foundation of self-love, self-compassion, and self-empowerment that improves our well-being and enriches our lives when we make self-care a priority in our daily routine. Amidst the bustle and noise of daily life, we may create a sanctuary of peace and tranquility that nurtures our body, mind, and spirit with the healing balm of self-care by setting apart moments of calm, seclusion, and self-reflection.

Basically, promoting physical well-being is a complex tapestry of exercise, eating right, getting enough sleep, and taking care of oneself that intertwines resilience, health, and energy into a harmonic whole. This path honors the sacred temple of our bodies as a vehicle of power, energy, and grace, and celebrates the interdependence of mind, body, and spirit. Through intentional, aware, and loving care of our physical health, we create an abundant, joyful, and vibrant existence that shines from the inside out.

May we embrace the transformative power of self-care and nourishment as we set out on the journey of nourishing our physical well-being, approaching it with curiosity, compassion, and an adventurous spirit that calls us to explore the depths of our physicality and connect with the wisdom of our bodies. Knowing that physical well-being is not a goal but a sacred journey of self-discovery, growth, and transformation that leads to a life of vitality, balance, and flourishing on all levels of our being, may we dance with joy, eat with gratitude, rest with ease, and take care of ourselves with love.

Cultivating Mental Resilience

Among the many trials and happy moments that make up life, mental resilience is one trait that sticks out as a source of courage and strength. It is the skill of skillfully negotiating the rough waters of misfortune with bravery, grace, and unflinching resolve. Mental resilience enables us to rise above setbacks and emerge stronger, wiser, and more resilient than before, much like a solid oak tree that withstands the hardest of storms.

In order to develop mental resilience, one must be able to accept hardship as a transforming chance for personal development. Challenges don't have to be seen as insurmountable barriers; instead, we can choose to consider them as stepping stones toward empowerment and personal growth. Every obstacle, every failure, every adversity gives us an opportunity to grow, learn, and adjust, building a resilient attitude based on courage, optimism, and resilience.

Mental resilience is the ability to face life's issues head-on with a spirit of ingenuity, inner strength, and resilience rather than avoiding them or acting as though they don't exist. Even in the midst of uncertainty, fear, and doubt, we are driven onward by our ability to overcome adversity and weather life's storms with a strong sense of purpose and determination. Resilience helps us develop an attitude of unyielding tenacity and resolve, which gives us the courage, adaptability, and optimism to deal with life's bumps and turns.

Self-awareness is an essential component in developing a strong sense of inner strength, resilience, and clarity in the art of mental resilience cultivation. By practicing self-awareness, we can better understand our inner selves and build the ability to face difficulties head-on with fortitude, wisdom, and clarity. We also become more alert to our thoughts, feelings, and beliefs. The foundation of mental resilience is self-awareness, which allows us to identify and control our feelings, ideas, and behaviors in a positive and flexible way.

By engaging in activities like self-reflection, mindfulness, and meditation, we can develop a strong sense of self-awareness that improves our capacity to handle stress, fortify our resilience, and flourish in the face of hardship. We build mental resilience and cultivate an inner resource bank that helps us face life's obstacles with bravery, grace, and authenticity when we tune into our inner landscape with inquiry, compassion, and non-judgment.

Emotional intelligence becomes a beacon of hope in the art of building mental toughness, showing the way to increased self-awareness, empathy, and resilience. The ability to identify, comprehend, and regulate our own emotions as well as those of others with understanding, compassion, and honesty is referred to as emotional intelligence. We can develop the ability to negotiate challenging social situations, communicate clearly, and create enduring connections that promote our mental health and wellbeing by developing our emotional intelligence.

We may improve our emotional intelligence and strengthen our potential for resilience, empathy, and connection by engaging in skills like active listening, empathy, and emotional control. Gaining a deeper comprehension of our own feelings as well as those of others helps us to build empathy, compassion, and a sense of connectivity that promotes cooperation, fortitude, and support from one another when faced with hardship.

Positive psychology shows up as a potent paradigm for developing optimism, thankfulness, and resilience in the face of life's obstacles in the field of mental resilience. The focus of positive psychology is on developing positive feelings, attributes, and characteristics that improve our resilience, general well-being, and quality of life. We can develop optimism, thankfulness, and resilience that enable us to flourish in the midst of adversity by concentrating on our strengths, values, and goals.

We can use positive psychology to develop a resilient mentality based on hope, optimism, and self-efficacy by engaging in activities like gratitude journaling, positive affirmations, and strengths-based reflection. We may develop a sense of agency, optimism, and resilience that empowers us to meet life's obstacles with grace, courage, and resilience by concentrating on our innate abilities and resources.

Social support surfaces as a fundamental component of wellbeing, resilience, and thriving in the face of adversity in the art of building mental resilience. In times of stress, suffering, and adversity, social support refers to the web of people, connections, and communities that offer us practical, psychological, and emotional support. We may improve our general quality of life, mental toughness, and sense of belonging by fostering strong relationships, feeling like we belong, and asking for help when we need it.

We may establish a sense of connection, belonging, and support that improves our mental resilience, wellbeing, and sense of belonging by doing things like attending to friends, family, or support groups; volunteering; or taking part in group activities. By surrounding ourselves with a network of people who encourage, inspire, and empower us, we develop resilience, compassion, and a sense of interconnectivity that helps us get through the difficulties and hardships of life.

Developing mental resilience is essentially a life-changing process of self-awareness, development, and empowerment that gives us the ability to face obstacles head-on with bravery, grace, and steadfast resolve. We may establish a resilient mindset that enables us to thrive in the face of uncertainty, change, and adversity by employing positive psychology, embracing adversity as a chance for growth, cultivating self-awareness, developing emotional intelligence, and fostering social support. We can develop an inner sense of strength, bravery, and wisdom that empowers us to overcome life's obstacles and come out stronger, smarter, and more resilient than before by mastering the art of mental resilience cultivation.

CHAPTER 3
Managing Stress and Prioritizing Self-Care

As we set out on the complex adventure that is life, we become enmeshed in the fine dance of stress management and self-care prioritization. This tightrope walk, or balancing act, between the demands of the outside world and our inner needs calls for dexterity, awareness, and a strong dedication to promoting our wellbeing. In the fast-paced world of today, when stress is all around us and self-care is frequently neglected, seeking balance turns into a significant artistic endeavor that fortifies our inner calm, vigor, and resilience.

Stress is an inescapable force that permeates all aspect of our life and can be both an ally and an enemy. While a certain level of stress can serve as a motivator and stimulant for development, chronic stress's corrosive hold can sap our energy, impair our judgment, and throw off our sense of balance. In order to properly manage stress, we must embrace self-awareness, resilience, and adaptive coping mechanisms that enable us to face life's obstacles head-on with courage and grace.

The development of good coping mechanisms that allow us to control our emotions, thoughts, and behaviors in the face of difficulty is essential to the art of stress management. These coping mechanisms, which can be achieved through artistic expression, movement, deep breathing techniques, or mindfulness meditation, act as mooring points of stability amidst the turbulent waves of stress. We can harness the force of resilience and inner strength that keeps us going through the ups and downs of life by intentionally and carefully caring to our inner landscape.

Self-care appears as a bright thread in the stress management fabric that permeates our whole wellbeing and illuminates our path with vitality, joy, and wholeness. Self-care is a sacred commitment to sustaining our mind, body, and spirit; it is not a luxury. It replenishes our reserves and cultivates a profound sense of acceptance and love for ourselves. Setting limits, attending to our needs, and dedicating special time for pursuits that refuel, revitalize, and restore our inner essence are all part of prioritizing self-care.

Self-care can take many different forms. It can involve taking care of our physical health with a healthy diet and regular exercise, as well as our mental health with relaxation, rest, and enjoyable activities. By partaking in activities that nourish our spirit and soul, including times of silence, intimacy, and self-expression, we refuel our batteries and develop an inner peace that spills over into the outer world.

Mindfulness shines as a guiding light in the delicate art of striking a balance between stress management and self-care, illuminating our path with present, awareness, and acceptance. By encouraging us to live in the present with curiosity, openness, and non-judgment, mindfulness enables us to see our inner landscape as it develops with compassion and clarity. We develop a sense of inner calm, resiliency, and composure by grounding ourselves in the present, which enables us to handle life's obstacles with poise and knowledge.

By incorporating mindfulness exercises like meditation, mindful movement, or conscious breathing into our daily routine, we may strengthen our connection to the richness of each moment and develop a sense of vitality and groundedness that helps us get through life's ups and downs. We can become more in tune with our inner rhythm and develop a profound feeling of self-awareness and present that supports our resilience by tuning into the symphony of our breath, sensations, and emotions.

Building strong boundaries and practicing self-compassion become pillars of strength that sustain us during the ups and downs of life's struggles. Establishing boundaries entails identifying our boundaries, respecting our needs, and standing up for our wellbeing in a world that frequently demands our time and effort. We make room for self-care, relaxation, and rejuvenation that feeds our souls and uplifts our spirits when we set clear and compassionate boundaries.

Resilience, self-worth, and inner serenity are fostered by practicing self-compassion, which is the delicate art of treating oneself with kindness, understanding, and acceptance. By warmly and empathetically accepting our flaws, weaknesses, and challenges, we develop a strong sense of self-compassion that gets us through life's ups and downs and fosters a sense of acceptance, completeness, and self-love.

Adopting a mentality of curiosity, flexibility, and adaptation becomes the cornerstone of our resilience and growth in the complex dance of stress management and self-care priorities. By taking on life's obstacles with an open mind and an open heart, we develop a curiosity that pushes us to investigate, discover, and develop from our experiences. By embracing flexibility and adaptation, we respond to change with creativity, resourcefulness, and resilience, and we gracefully and ingeniously navigate life's curveballs.

The ability to manage stress while also taking care of oneself is ultimately a profound path of empowerment, self-discovery, and progress that happens with every breath and step we take. Carefully caring to our inner garden and cultivating resilience, self-compassion, and mindfulness seeds helps us create a beautiful tapestry of well-being that helps us weather life's storms. We learn the skill of living with intention, grace, and inner peace via the delicate dance of stress management and self-care prioritization. We also appreciate the holy temple of our being with the kindness and care it deserves.

Understanding Stress

Stress is the silent conductor of chaos in our lives' symphony. It is a complex phenomenon that can ambush us without warning, resembling a cunning animal poised to strike. With its fast-paced demands and ever rising expectations, the modern world has become an ideal environment for stress to grow and take many different forms. Comprehending stress means going into its depths, working out its nuances, and figuring out how it affects our mental, emotional, and physical health.

It is fundamentally a physiological reaction that is brought on by our body's built-in survival strategy. Our brain triggers a series of hormonal and metabolic reactions that release cortisol and adrenaline into the bloodstream in response to perceived threats or challenges. This "fight or flight" response readies our body for action and increased awareness, readying us to either meet the threat head-on or run for safety.

Although our ancestors found great benefit from this instinctive reaction when faced with impending danger, in the contemporary world, where stressors frequently take on more subdued and prolonged forms, this adaptive process might have unintended consequences. Chronically triggering our stress response can result in a variety of medical conditions, both mental and physical, from burnout and anxiety disorders to compromised immunity and cardiovascular problems.

Stress can come from a wide range of situations in our life, including job, relationships, money, health, and more. These sources of stress are as varied as the colors of the rainbow. Stress can be caused by a wide range of factors, from financial strains and tense interpersonal relationships to impending deadlines and demanding supervisors. Furthermore, internal variables that lead to a vicious cycle of self-perpetuating angst include perfectionism, self-doubt, and negative self-talk can further amplify stress levels.

Understanding how perception affects how we react to stressors is crucial as we attempt to navigate the maze of stress. The perspective and meaning we give to obstacles can have a big impact on how stressed out we get. The fact that different people may view the same obstacle as a manageable challenge or an impassable mountain emphasizes the subjective nature of stress and how it affects our overall health.

More importantly, how well we traverse turbulent seas is largely dependent on our coping mechanisms and stress-resilience. While some people employ constructive ways to release their stress, like working out, practicing meditation, or engaging in creative endeavors, others may adopt unhealthy coping mechanisms like substance abuse, procrastination, or emotional eating. To protect our wellbeing and build resilience in the face of adversity, it is essential to comprehend our coping strategies and create healthier stress management practices.

Moreover, the mind-body connection is an essential component of the complex network relating to stress and wellbeing. The interaction of our feelings, ideas, and bodily experiences can produce a feedback loop that can either increase or decrease the negative effects of stress on our bodies and minds. The cycle of rumination and suffering that frequently accompanies chronic stress can be broken by engaging in practices like mindfulness, cognitive reframing, and relaxation techniques. These can help us create an inner peace and balance.

Building self-awareness shows up as a lighthouse in the field of stress management, guiding us through the labyrinth of stressors and triggers. We can better understand the thought, feeling, and behavior patterns that raise our stress levels by tuning into our inner landscape with compassion and curiosity. Being self-aware gives us the ability to pinpoint the sources of our stress and deal with them, which gives us a sense of agency and control over our wellbeing.

Creating a strong support system of friends, family, or mental health specialists can also act as a diversion from stress and offer a secure environment for communication and validation. In addition to reducing feelings of overwhelm and isolation, interacting with others, talking about our problems, and asking for help when we need it can help us feel resilient and like we belong in the midst of difficulty.

Self-care shows up as a lifeline that helps us get through the ups and downs of life when we're under stress. By self-compassion, relaxation, and engaging in joyful activities, we may take care of our physical, mental, and spiritual well-being, recharging our batteries and strengthening our resilience in the face of stress. Setting self-care as a top priority is a holy commitment to recognizing our needs and providing loving, caring care for our inner essence, not a sign of selfishness.

Adopting a growth mindset becomes a fundamental tenet of our resilience and wellbeing in the pursuit of understanding stress. When we see problems as chances for development and learning rather than as insurmountable hurdles, we are more equipped to develop optimism and resourcefulness when faced with hardship. Adopting a growth mindset gives us the flexibility, inventiveness, and sense of empowerment to deal with the challenges of stress in a way that moves us closer to our goals of personal development and fulfillment.

Understanding stress is essentially a path of self-awareness, development, and empowerment that asks us to accept the complexity of our nature with grace and resiliency. Through exploring the depths of stress, releasing its entanglements, and intentionally tending to our well-being, we can develop an inner sense of vitality and serenity that carries us through the ups and downs of life. May we weave resilience, self-compassion, and mindfulness into the fabric of stress and wellbeing, so that it becomes a vivid mosaic of wholeness and harmony that reaches out into the world.

Techniques for Stress Management

Stress-reduction strategies are like the calming tunes that balance out life's chaos, bringing us through hard patches with grace and resiliency. Each person is the conductor of the stress symphony, arranging a melody of self-care, mindfulness, and resilience to get through the challenges of contemporary life. Adopting a holistic perspective on stress management entails piecing together a complex web of techniques that support the body, mind, and spirit while encouraging equilibrium and wellbeing in the face of adversity.

The practice of mindfulness is one of the cornerstones of efficient stress management. By encouraging us to ground ourselves in the here and now, mindfulness helps us develop a sense of presence and awareness that cuts through the cacophony of our rushing thoughts and anxieties. We may educate our minds to notice thoughts and feelings without passing judgment by using techniques like deep breathing, body scans, and meditation. This will allow us to create space for clarity and serenity in the middle of a stressful situation. By practicing mindfulness, we build a haven within ourselves—a resilient haven of calm—that supports us through the ups and downs of life.

In the alchemy of stress management, exercise proves to be a powerful remedy, utilizing movement's ability to reduce tension, increase endorphins, and revitalize our bodies and minds. Regular exercise, whether it be in the form of yoga, dance, or outdoor pursuits, can be a spiritual healer, reviving our energy and fortifying our ability to handle stress. Movement with a rhythmic cadence transforms into a dance of regeneration and release, releasing us from the bonds of stress and reviving our spirits with power and vitality.

In the temple of stress management, self-care is elevated to a sacred ritual that calls us to honor our needs and provide compassionate, loving care for our wellbeing. Self-care is a range of activities that refuel our bodies and strengthen our resistance to stress, such as taking a relaxing bath or enjoying a hearty meal. Making self-care a priority helps us regain control over our health and cultivates a sense of harmony and balance that helps us weather the ups and downs of life.

The practice of relaxation offers a haven of calm and tranquility in the middle of the hectic pace of everyday life. It is a profound expression of self-care and stress management. Techniques such as progressive muscle relaxation, guided imagery, and aromatherapy can help to calm the mind, relax the nervous system, and bring our bodies back into balance. We can build islands of calm amid the sea of stress by scheduling times of relaxation and peace into our daily schedules. This allows us to gently and calmly nurture our well-being.

The road to empowerment and perseverance in the face of adversity is illuminated by cultivating a growth mentality. It gives us the strength and optimism to face the intricacies of stress head-on by seeing problems as chances for development and education rather than as impassable barriers. Adopting a growth mindset empowers us to take charge of our lives, realizing our inherent capacity to triumph over hardship and thrive in the face of life's challenges. We can develop a sense of agency and resilience that drives us toward personal improvement and fulfillment by adopting a growth mindset.

In the world of stress management, community and connection provide a haven of affirmation and support, creating a sense of unity and belonging in the face of adversity. Creating a strong support system of friends, family, or mental health specialists can be a lifesaver of compassion and understanding, giving a secure environment for communication and recovery. Making connections with people, opening up to them about our difficulties, and asking for help when we need it feeds our souls, strengthening our ability to bounce back from setbacks and maintaining our wellbeing.

In the field of stress management, the path of self-discovery presents itself as a holy quest that beckons us to delve into the core of our being with compassion and inquiry. Through practicing mindfulness and introspection, we can gently tune into our inner landscape and uncover the thought, emotion, and behavior patterns that influence our stress experience. Self-discovery turns into a doorway to change and empowerment, enabling us to take back our stories, get over self-limiting ideas, and develop inner calm and honesty in the face of adversity.

When it comes to stress management, creativity becomes a very useful ally because it provides a platform for self-expression and investigation that goes beyond language and reason. Whether via writing, painting, or music, creative endeavors can be a cathartic way to release tension and open doors to inner healing and tranquility. By releasing us from the bonds of tension and releasing the limitless possibilities of our imagination and soul, the act of creativity transforms into a dance of liberation and regeneration.

In the context of stress management, accepting the essence of thankfulness becomes a transforming activity that invites us to develop an appreciation and perspective in the face of life's obstacles. By appreciating all of life's blessings, no matter how tiny, we change our perspective from one of scarcity to abundance and thankfulness. Gratitude becomes a lighthouse that shines on the stress-causing shadows, encouraging a resilient and contented spirit that helps us get through life's ups and downs.

Curiosity turns into a compass that shows the way through the maze of stress management and leads to self-awareness and personal development. We can uncover the layers of our being with humility and understanding when we approach our experiences with open minds and amazement, which fosters a continuous process of self-discovery and transformation. When we welcome the secrets of our inner world with grace and bravery, curiosity opens the door to empowerment and liberation.

Laughter is a powerful tool in the complex dance of stress management. It fills us with joy and lightness and casts a radiance of humor and mirth over the shadows of tension. Through embracing lighthearted and playful moments, we improve our mood, change our viewpoint, and recover a sense of humor in the face of life's obstacles. Laughter serves as a conduit to our true selves, reminding us of the resiliency and vigor that are buried deep within us.

Learning how to create boundaries becomes essential to managing stress because it gives us the confidence to stand up for what we need and defend our health in a confident and self-assured manner. We build a haven of safety and independence that protects us from the assault of stress and anxiety when we set clear boundaries in our relationships and obligations. Setting boundaries cultivates a sense of balance and empowerment that gets us through the ups and downs of life. It also becomes a statement of self-worth and self-care.

In the orchestration of stress management, embracing the rhythm of rest and rejuvenation becomes a spiritual practice that invites us to respect the ebb and flow of our inherent vitality and energy. We refuel, regain equilibrium, and strengthen our ability to withstand stress by scheduling regular times for relaxation, introspection, and renewal. Rest becomes a place of rebirth and rejuvenation where our spirits are nurtured with the gift of restoration and tranquility.

A journey of self-discovery, development, and empowerment, stress management invites us to accept the complexity of our humanity with grace and resiliency. Through exploring the depths of stress, releasing its entanglements, and intentionally tending to our well-being, we can develop an inner sense of vitality and serenity that carries us through the ups and downs of life. May we weave resilience, self-compassion, and mindfulness into the fabric of stress and wellbeing, so that it becomes a vivid mosaic of wholeness and harmony that reaches out into the world.

Importance of Self-Care Practices

Self-care routines are the soft murmurs of self-love that envelop our spirits in a cocoon of warmth and sustenance. These are the holy rites that uplift our souls, strengthen our will to survive, and show us the way to inner serenity and wellbeing. Self-care appears as the North Star directing us back to ourselves in the chaotic and demanding world of modern life, reminding us to tend to our needs with kindness and intention.

Fundamental to self-care is a deep understanding of our intrinsic worth and value. It is a bold act of self-love and respect that acknowledges the sanctity of our existence and declares that we are worthy of love, care, and nurturing. By making self-care routines a priority, we demonstrate our dedication to respecting our mental, emotional, and spiritual health and recognizing that our needs are important and should be given the care and attention they require.

Self-care is a dance of harmony and balance that invites us to attentively and sensitively tune into the rhythms of our bodies and minds. It is a symphony of relaxation and renewal, motion and calm, sustenance and pleasure that balances the discord of everyday existence. By engaging in self-care activities, we strengthen our resilience and develop a sense of balance and vitality that helps us face life's obstacles head-on. This enables us to ride the ups and downs with grace and sincerity.

A fundamental component of self-care practices that honor the innate knowledge of our physical beings is taking care of our bodies by providing them with healthy nutrition, enough sleep, and physical activity. We reaffirm our commitment to caring for the vessel that carries us through life with strength and vitality when we eat it healthful meals that energize and nourish it, when we respect our need for rest and relaxation, and when we move in ways that excite and invigorate it.

Self-care is a broad concept that encompasses not just physical health but also mental and emotional well-being. It is a patchwork of techniques that develop resilience to life's difficulties, self-awareness, and emotional intelligence. We take good care of the garden of our minds by planting seeds of self-awareness, compassion, and growth that grow into the brilliant blossoms of inner peace and emotional balance through mindfulness, meditation, journaling, or therapy.

In order to promote joy, play, and self-expression, creativity emerges as a sacred expression of self-care, inviting us to draw from the reservoir of our imagination and intuition. Taking up artistic, musical, literary, or dancing endeavors opens doors to healing and self-discovery since they provide a safe haven for expression and investigation outside the bounds of language and reason. Creating becomes a dance of release and rejuvenation, releasing us from the bonds of tension and bringing the vivid colors of inspiration and life into our bodies.

In the tapestry of self-care practices, connection and community provide a lifeline of support and solidarity, promoting a sense of belonging, empathy, and understanding throughout life's hardships. Establishing genuine connections, looking for help, and talking about our difficulties with reliable friends nourishes our spirits, increases our resilience, and improves our general wellbeing. As a reminder that we are not traveling alone and that, alongside each other, we can withstand life's storms with grace and fortitude, connection becomes a healing salve for the heart.

In the alchemy of self-care, mindfulness emerges as a powerful potion that grounds us in the present and invites us to develop an awareness, acceptance, and presence. In the midst of the chaos of everyday life, we can make room for clarity, peace, and tranquility by tuning into our thoughts, feelings, and sensations with inquiry and non-judgment. In the face of life's uncertainties and difficulties, mindfulness turns into a haven of serenity and resilience, a place of stillness and introspection.

Setting boundaries gives us the ability to respect and be forceful in addressing our needs, values, and limitations. It also becomes a fundamental component of self-care techniques. Establishing boundaries in our relationships, obligations, and self-care practices helps us to build a secure haven of independence and safety that protects us from the overwhelming waves of stress. Setting boundaries cultivates a sense of balance and empowerment that gets us through the ups and downs of life. It also becomes a statement of self-worth and self-care.

In the self-care garden, gratitude emerges as a transforming practice that invites us to cultivate a sense of appreciation, abundance, and perspective among life's challenges. By recognizing and appreciating all of life's blessings, no matter how great or small, we change our perspective from one of scarcity to one of thankfulness and abundance. Gratitude turns into a powerful potion that nourishes our spirits and builds a resilient, joyful, and contented feeling of self-worth that helps us weather the ups and downs of life.

Curiosity serves as a compass in negotiating the maze of self-care routines, illuminating the way to personal empowerment, progress, and self-discovery. We can unravel the secrets of our inner worlds with humility and insight when we approach our experiences with open minds and amazement, which fosters a continuous process of self-awareness and transformation. Curiosity turns into a lighthouse that kindles our inner sparks of creativity, curiosity, and resilience, giving us the strength and grace to bravely and gracefully accept the complexity of our humanity.

Laughter appears like a bright sun, piercing the stress-filled clouds with golden rays of pleasure, joy, and lightness. Through embracing lightheartedness, humor, and playfulness, we can improve our mood, change our viewpoint, and recover a sense of humor even in the face of life's obstacles. Laughter serves as a conduit to our true selves, bringing to light the resiliency, vigor, and joy that are inherent in our beings.

Self-care routines are the soft murmurs of self-love that envelop our spirits in a cocoon of warmth and sustenance. These are the holy rites that uplift our souls, strengthen our will to survive, and show us the way to inner serenity and wellbeing. Self-care appears as the North Star directing us back to ourselves in the chaotic and demanding world of modern life, reminding us to tend to our needs with kindness and intention.

CHAPTER 4
Fueling Your Body and Mind

Our bodies and brains are built on the fundamental cornerstone of nutrition, a symphony of flavors, colors, and nutrients that create a tapestry of vitality and wellbeing. Each meal we consume is a brushstroke painting an image of health and sustenance, much like a professional chef creating a work of art. Nutrition is the maestro who orchestrates the harmony between food and body, mind, and soul in the gastronomic dance of life.

The palette of nutritious meals brimming with nutrients that sustain life and give our bodies and brains energy and vitality is the rich and varied canvas that is nutrition. The fundamental components of human health are fruits, vegetables, whole grains, lean proteins, and healthy fats; together, they create a rainbow of tastes and textures that entice our senses and provide energy to our bodies. Every mouthful is an ode to the abundance of nature, a gift of sustenance that keeps our bodies and souls going.

Food becomes medicine for both the body and the spirit thanks to the alchemy of nutrition, which extends beyond simple sustenance and into the fields of healing and renewal. The vivid colors of fruits and vegetables indicate that they contain antioxidants, vitamins, and minerals that shield our cells from inflammation and oxidative stress, boosting our defenses against illness. The brain benefits from the nourishing elixir of omega-3 fatty acids, which are present in nuts and fatty fish. These fatty acids improve mental clarity, emotional control, and cognitive performance.

In the field of nutrition, mindful eating is emerging as a spiritual practice that invites us to tune into our hunger, satiety, and pleasure sensations, which inform our food choices and eating patterns, and to savor each meal with reverence and thanks. We nurture not just our bodies but also our spirits by practicing awareness and presence at the table, which creates a stronger bond with the food we eat and the nutrients it offers. Eating mindfully transforms into a moving meditation, a dance of appreciation and awareness that improves our connection to both food and ourselves.

A ritual of self-love and sustenance that treats our bodies and minds with respect and intention, nutrition takes on the role of self-care. We recognize our intrinsic value and merit when we choose foods that invigorate and nourish us, and we accept that we should be taken care of and cherished. Amidst the diverse array of self-care techniques, diet stands out as a fundamental element that enhances our ability to bounce back from setbacks, maintains our energy, and gives us the confidence to face life's obstacles head-on.

The language of nutrition speaks to our emotional and mental landscapes as well as the physical, providing a means of recovery, development, and metamorphosis. The gut-brain link highlights the tremendous influence of diet on our mood, cognition, and emotional balance while shedding light on the complex interaction between our digestive health and mental health. Through the use of foods that promote gut health and brain function, we can develop mental clarity, inner serenity, and emotional resilience that help us stay rooted in the chaos of everyday life.

Through the power of food and lifestyle choices, nutrition as nourishment becomes a voyage of investigation and discovery, a quest to unlock the secrets of optimal health and well-being. The age-old knowledge of Traditional Chinese Medicine and Ayurveda weaves a tapestry of holistic treatment, directing us to respect our individual constitutions, harmonize with nature's rhythms, and feed our bodies foods that are tailored to our own requirements and tastes. Regaining our natural capacity to heal and thrive via the alchemy of food and lifestyle, we set out on a journey of self-discovery and empowerment by accepting the wisdom of conventional healing systems.

Even the most discriminating eater may become confused and overwhelmed by the abundance of trends, diets, and contradicting advice that characterizes the modern nutrition scene. The deluge of dietary recommendations, ranging from paleo to keto, vegan to intermittent fasting, frequently masks the obvious fact that nutrition is a very personal and unique experience that goes beyond universal guidelines. We reclaim our agency and autonomy in the area of nutrition by acknowledging our bodies' knowledge, listening to our appetites and instincts, and approaching food with curiosity and openness. This allows us to have a nourishing relationship with food that is tailored to our individual needs and tastes.

Inviting us to investigate the rich tapestry of culinary traditions and flavors that grace the world table, nutrition as nourishment is a celebration of diversity, creativity, and plenty. The world is a great banquet of sensations and fragrances that invite us to savor and delight in the richness of cultural diversity and gastronomic heritage, from the street cafes of Morocco to the noodle stalls of Japan, the spice markets of India to the olive fields of Greece. We broaden our palates, add to our culinary skills, and satiate our bodies and minds with the variety of nutrients and phytochemicals that support our health and vitality when we embrace the flavors of the world.

Balance appears as a guiding element in the mosaic of nutrition as nourishment, balancing the yin and yang of food and life, indulgence and restraint, pleasure and discipline. By adopting a balanced eating strategy, we may cultivate a sense of moderation and mindfulness that supports our health and well-being while honoring our wants and desires and honoring our bodies' signals of hunger and fullness. Balance turns into a touchstone that helps us stay grounded in the here and now and helps us make thoughtful decisions that wisely and gracefully nourish our bodies and minds.

Gratitude blossoms as a transforming practice that infuses each bite with appreciation, abundance, and joy in the context of nutrition as nourishment. We respect the labor of love that goes into every piece of food, from seed to table, by appreciating the flavors, textures, and fragrances of our meals with gratitude and presence. Gratitude transforms into a nourishing potion that enhances our dining experience and cultivates a mindfulness, community, and connection that benefits our bodies and spirits equally.

We reclaim our power as mindful eaters in the dance of nutrition as nourishment, respecting the tremendous effects of food on our bodies, brains, and spirits. By practicing self-care, mindful eating, and a well-rounded nutritional approach, we can attain optimal health and well-being by nourishing ourselves with love, intention, and reverence. Let us feast on the abundance of nature's offerings at the banquet of life, cherishing every morsel as a prayer of thanksgiving, a celebration of life, and an evidence of the transforming potential of food as sustenance.

The Function of Nutrients in Health

The unsung heroes of our daily existence are the nutrients, who silently operate in the background to provide resilience and energy to our bodies, minds, and souls. Nutrients play a crucial role in the complex dance of wellness, providing the building blocks that allow every cell, tissue, and organ to function and sustain our health and well-being. Similar to a conductor of a symphony orchestra creating a beautiful melody, nutrients are essential to the complex equilibrium that maintains our mental, emotional, and physical well-being.

Nutrients have a key role in nourishing our bodies from the inside out, which is at the core of wellness. Water, vitamins, minerals, proteins, carbs, fats, and carbohydrates all combine to form a symphony of nourishment, with each component contributing in a special way to the overall composition of wellness. Minerals and vitamins assist cellular activity and metabolic processes by functioning as necessary co-factors in enzyme reactions. The building blocks of life, proteins are responsible for the regeneration and repair of muscles, tissues, and organs. Our bodies run on fuel from carbohydrates, while lipids are essential for maintaining hormone balance, cellular integrity, and cognitive function. The elixir of life, water, ensures maximum function and vitality by hydrating and cleansing our bodies.

Nutrients play a role in wellness that goes beyond simple nutrition to include a whole-person approach to health that nourishes the body, mind, and spirit. A wellness-centered diet is built around nutrient-dense foods including fruits, vegetables, whole grains, legumes, nuts, and seeds. These foods offer a wealth of vitamins, minerals, antioxidants, and phytonutrients that promote optimum health and vitality. By providing our bodies with a wide variety of vibrant, nutrient-dense foods, we can boost cognitive performance, build stronger immune systems, and improve our general health.

Nutrients are strong partners in the complex web of wellness, helping to prevent and treat chronic illnesses and disorders. Antioxidants present in fruits and vegetables have anti-inflammatory qualities that shield our cells from oxidative stress and inflammation, lowering our chance of developing chronic illnesses like cancer, diabetes, and heart disease. Rich in fatty fish, flaxseeds, and walnuts, omega-3 fatty acids have strong anti-inflammatory properties that promote joint, brain, and cardiovascular health. Foods high in fiber aid in blood sugar regulation, healthy digestion, and weight management while lowering the risk of diseases like obesity, diabetes, and constipation.

Emerging research has demonstrated the impact of diet on mood, cognition, and emotional balance, underscoring the equally significant role that nutrients play in mental wellness. The gut-brain connection highlights the complex interrelationship between mental health and gut health, emphasizing the necessity of nutrition in maintaining both brain function and a healthy microbiota. Probiotic-rich foods, like yogurt, kefir, and fermented veggies, improve the production of serotonin, the "feel-good" neurotransmitter, which supports mental health by nourishing our gut flora. Whole grains, leafy greens, and legumes are good sources of B vitamins, which are essential for the production of serotonin and dopamine, which supports mood control and cognitive function.

In addition to providing physical nourishment, nutrients also support our mental and spiritual health, promoting a strong feeling of self-worth, purpose, and connection. Through mindful eating, we may appreciate the love and labor that goes into growing our food and the sustenance it offers by savoring each bite with awareness and appreciation. A greater appreciation for nature's offerings and the interdependence of all living things can be fostered by approaching food with intention, presence, and reverence. Sharing meals with family and friends transforms into a holy ritual of celebration and communion that feeds our spirits just as much as our bodies by creating a sense of joy, connection, and belonging.

Nutrients are like catalysts for change in the field of holistic wellness; they lead us on a path of self-awareness, recovery, and development. The age-old knowledge found in conventional medical systems like Ayurveda and Traditional Chinese Medicine provides a road map for balancing nutrients in a harmonious way, respecting our distinct constitutions, and synchronizing with the cycles of nature to support our specific health needs. We may use the healing power of food to reestablish equilibrium, energy, and resilience in the body, mind, and spirit by adhering to the concepts of harmony, balance, and seasonally appropriate diet.

By encouraging us to take charge of our health and well-being through deliberate dietary decisions and lifestyle choices, the language of nutrients in wellness speaks to us of agency, empowerment, and self-care. We reclaim our power as conscientious consumers and stewards of our bodies by emphasizing nutrient-dense meals, mindful eating, and self-care rituals. We also respect the significant influence of nutrition on our physical, mental, and emotional wellness. Every meal becomes a time to nourish ourselves with love, intention, and appreciation, creating a deep sense of well-being that radiates from within. From the vivid hues of a rainbow salad to the comforting warmth of a nutritious soup.

Nutrients are like the maestro orchestrating the harmonic interplay of food, body, mind, and spirit in the symphony of wellbeing. Honoring the transforming potential of nutrition in sustaining our bodies, brains, and souls helps us achieve optimal resilience, health, and vitality that go beyond physical well-being. We reaffirm our commitment to lovingly, intentionally, and reverently feeding ourselves with every nutrient-rich meal we savor and mindful mouthful we take, cultivating a profound sense of well-being that blossoms from within and radiates outward into the world.

Healthy Eating Habits

A lively and meaningful existence is largely dependent on having healthy eating habits, which nurture not only our bodies but also our minds and spirits. These behaviors are rooted in a respect for Mother Nature's bountiful offerings, a harmonic dance with the seasons, and a profound connection to the earth's inherent cycles. Adopting a healthy diet is a holistic strategy that recognizes the complex interrelationships between food, health, and well-being. It goes beyond simply counting calories and minerals.

Variety is essential to creating a harmonious eating pattern. Our plates should be a vivid canvas of colors and textures, much way a rainbow displays a kaleidoscope of colors. We satisfy our palates and provide our bodies with a range of vitamins, minerals, antioxidants, and phytonutrients by include a variety of fruits, vegetables, whole grains, legumes, nuts, and seeds. From the beta-carotene-rich orange of carrots to the antioxidant-rich purple of blueberries, each color offers a distinct set of health advantages that work together to assist our immune system, support digestive health, and increase general vigor.

Intention and mindfulness set the pace for good eating. We can relish every bite, enjoy the flavors and textures, and pay attention to our bodies' signals of hunger and fullness when we eat mindfully and in the moment. Eating mindfully involves paying attention to our bodies, respecting their wisdom, and taking care of our mental and spiritual well-being in addition to our bodily needs. We can escape the cycle of thoughtless eating, emotional triggers, and outside distractions by developing a mindful connection with food and learning to cherish each meal as a sacred time for self-care and sustenance.

The secret to long-lasting, healthful eating habits is balance. Our bodies function best with a balanced combination of macronutrients, such as carbohydrates, proteins, and fats. This is analogous to how a symphony needs a harmonious combination of instruments to generate a beautiful tune. Our bodies use carbohydrates as an energy source, proteins to construct and repair tissues, and lipids to produce hormones and maintain the health of our brains. By selecting meals that are complete, minimally processed, and provide a balance of these macronutrients, we provide our bodies with the fundamental building blocks they require to flourish.

The seasons determine the tempo of good eating practices. In the same way that nature provides an abundance of fresh food during the spring and summer, and substantial root vegetables throughout the fall and winter, our meals can be synchronized with the seasonal harvests to enhance our overall health and energy levels. Eating in accordance with the seasons promotes our bodies' natural cycles and rhythms and lets us take advantage of the fruits and vegetables' optimal flavor and nutritious content. We may acknowledge the wisdom of traditional eating customs, strengthen our connection to the land, and nourish ourselves in balance with the changing seasons by learning to read nature's seasonal signs.

A key element of good eating habits is flexibility. To create a seamless and dynamic musical experience, a symphony conductor modifies the tempo and dynamics of a performance. Similarly, we need to be flexible and sensitive to the evolving needs of our bodies and lifestyles. Eating with flexibility is paying attention to our bodies' signals of hunger and fullness, recognizing our cravings in moderation and balance, and keeping an open mind to new foods and culinary adventures. In the kitchen and at the table, we may embrace the joy of experimentation, creativity, and self-discovery when we approach healthy eating with an attitude of inquiry and openness.

The people we surround ourselves with add to the harmony of good eating practices. Similar to how a symphony unites a varied group of artists to produce a beautiful work of music, having meals with family, friends, and neighbors improves the nutritious experience of eating. Eating together creates a common space for celebration, laughing, and discussion while also fostering a sense of connection, belonging, and joy. We feed our bodies with the warmth and sustenance of human connection when we assemble around the table with an open heart and a spirit of gratitude.

Sustainable healthy eating practices are built on the foundations of empowerment and education. Similar to how a conductor of a symphony orchestra leads and enables players to blend their unique talents into a harmonious whole, we too need to arm ourselves with the information, abilities, and tools necessary to make wise food decisions and develop a lifelong connection with a nutritious diet. By providing us with the knowledge and skills to understand food labels, shop smarter, and understand the science behind nutrition, nutrition education gives us the ability to take control of our health and wellbeing. We have the capacity to turn eating into a happy, empowering experience of self-care and self-discovery by improving our culinary and nutritional understanding.

Resilience and self-compassion are important ingredients in the elaborate orchestration of good eating habits. Similar like how a symphony could face unforeseen difficulties and interruptions, adopting a balanced diet is not always easy or straightforward. The key to navigating the ups and downs of the gastronomic journey is to cultivate a spirit of resilience, adaptation, and self-compassion. Life's responsibilities, anxieties, and temptations may derail us. We may develop a loving, nourishing relationship with food that honors our bodies and minds with grace and love by accepting imperfection, learning from failures, and approaching healthy eating with a spirit of self-kindness and patience.

A rich and lively symphony of wellbeing is created by the interweaving of mindfulness, diversity, balance, seasonality, flexibility, community, education, and resilience in the fabric of healthy eating habits. We may develop a satisfying and healthy relationship with food that feeds not just our bodies but also our minds and spirits by embracing these concepts with creativity, ingenuity, and an open heart. We are harmonizing with the symphony of well-being that reverberates inside us and radiates outward into the world as we tune into the rhythm of the earth, recognize the wisdom of our bodies, and celebrate the joy of communal dining.

Practices of Mindful Eating

A profound discipline, mindful eating goes beyond the act of eating; it is a path of self-discovery, connection, and nutrition that calls us to develop a profound awareness of our bodies, minds, and spirits. Fundamentally, mindful eating is about interacting with food in a way that respects the here and now, revels in the senses, and recognizes the relationship between our dietary decisions and overall wellbeing. Eating becomes a nourishing and transforming ritual through the practice of deep listening, a dance of gratitude, and a journey of self-love.

The key to mindful eating is presence, which is the practice of living in the present and using all of our senses to fully experience the act of eating. We make room for mindfulness to flourish when we approach our meals with presence, which enables us to appreciate the tastes, textures, scents, and colors of every bite. Eating mindfully is more than just enjoying food; it's about approaching each meal with awe and curiosity, as if it were a symphony for our taste receptors, bringing forth a range of emotions that feed our bodies as well as our souls.

The development of gratitude—a deep appreciation for the path food takes from seed to plate and the innumerable hands, hearts, and components that have contributed to the sustenance in front of us—is essential to the mindful eating practice. We celebrate the Earth, the farmers, the cooks, and the nutrients that strengthen our bodies when we recognize the interdependent web of relationships that supports our food system. Gratitude reminds us of the abundance and gifts that adorn our plates and our lives, imbuing each bite with a sense of reverence and appreciation.

Eating mindfully is also a self-awareness exercise; it's a mirror reflecting our inner lives, feelings, and eating habits. We can learn to trust and listen to our bodies' wisdom by becoming aware of our hunger and satiety signs. By encouraging us to investigate our emotional attachments, triggers, and desires to food, mindful eating helps us understand how we relate to self-care and feeding. Developing self-awareness allows us to embrace and love our flaws and vulnerabilities, and to act with compassion and nonjudgment toward ourselves.

The path to self-love that is mindful eating celebrates our bodies as holy objects deserving of sustenance, care, and respect. We nourish our emotional and spiritual selves in addition to our physical bodies when we approach eating with love and compassion. A self-nurturing practice, mindful eating serves as a reminder that caring for oneself is an act of reverence and love that permeates all area of our lives. We may change our relationship with food from one of limitation and guilt to one of abundance, joy, and liberation by practicing self-love.

The invitation to mindful eating is to slow down; to let go of the hurry and anxiety that frequently accompanies our meals and, instead, to savor each bite with purpose and mindfulness. By eating slowly and deliberately, we give our bodies the opportunity to detect satiety and contentment and enable us to completely experience the nourishment that food gives. In addition to improving digestion and nutrient absorption, slow eating strengthens our bond with the process of self-nourishment and cultivates a tranquil, harmonious, and balanced relationship with food.

Eating mindfully is a joyful habit that celebrates the joys and pleasures that food brings, as well as the richness and abundance that are all around us. We inject lightness and pleasure into our eating experience by approaching meals with a spirit of playfulness and joy, bringing laughter, thankfulness, and appreciation to the table. Eating with joy serves as a reminder that food is more than just physical nourishment—rather, it is a source of inspiration, fun, and community that nourishes and elevates our spirits.

A voyage of connection, mindful eating serves as a link between us and the natural cycles, the web of life, and the earth's rhythms. We become one with the natural environment and weave our dietary decisions into its fabric by respecting the seasons, harvests, and the knowledge of ancient food practices. Eating mindfully is a celebration of the complex dance of life that keeps us all alive, a call to care and respect for the Earth, and a reminder of our interconnectedness with all beings.

Slowness, joy, connection, self-love, self-awareness, present, and gratitude all come together in mindful eating practices to produce a nourishing and transforming experience that affects not just our bodies but also our hearts and souls. Our lives and the lives of those around us are enhanced when we embrace the practice of mindful eating with openness, curiosity, and reverence. This is a spiritual journey of self-discovery, healing, and empowerment. We join the endless dance of sustenance, love, and interconnectedness that binds us all in the symphony of life as we savor each bite with mindfulness and intention, tuning into the melody of well-being that resonates inside us.

CHAPTER 5
The Power of Movement

A road of life, joy, and fulfillment is shown to us by the power of movement, which shines brightly in a world of hurry and bustle and time that seems to slide through our fingers like sand. Our bodies are complex machinery made of bone and flesh that are meant to move, stretch, and dance to the beat of life. Movement is the tune in the symphony of existence that coordinates our mental, emotional, and physical health and provides us with a path to empowerment, self-discovery, and transformation.

A small step toward movement and the release of our bodies from the bonds of inertia and stagnation is the first step towards achieving fitness and fulfillment. Exercise is more than just burning calories and toning muscles; it's a celebration of the wonders of our bodies, a nod to the power and mobility that allow us to move through the world with grace and assurance. By moving, we pay homage to the innate intelligence of our bodies—we pay attention to the subtle cues that come from our bones, muscles, and breath that point us in the direction of vitality, balance, and health.

Movement is powerful because of its profound effects on our minds and souls, in addition to its bodily benefits. Through physical activity, we reawaken latent energy within ourselves that ignite the inspiration, passion, and creativity that fuel our goals and dreams. As a kind of meditation, movement opens the door to mindfulness, presence, and inner serenity, enabling us to listen into our souls' whispers and block out the sounds of the outside world. We discover comfort, understanding, and a connection to our most fundamental selves in the dance of movement, which opens the door to introspection and personal development.

Fitness and contentment are journeys rather than goals, and movement is our devoted companion and guide on these adventures. Every stride, breath, and stretch we do is evidence of our dedication to self-love, self-care, and self-empowerment. We may sculpt our bodies, minds, and spirits into works of power, resilience, and beauty by using the rhythm of movement as a canvas for self-expression, a healing refuge, and a source of vitality.

Movement has a force that goes beyond the physical world and touches the depths of our spirits and emotions, agitating the waters of our hearts and souls. We let go of repressed feelings, anxieties, and tensions via movement dance, enabling them to flow from our bodies like a river heading toward the ocean. To be free from the bonds of self-doubt, insecurity, and restriction that confine us and keep us tiny and motionless is to move. Through movement, we embrace the infinite possibilities that lie ahead of us and break free to soar and expand into the endless expanse of our true potential.

Fitness and fulfillment are not distinct concepts; rather, they are woven throughout our lives, creating a narrative of resiliency, self-determination, and metamorphosis. Our bodies become temples of power, our minds become strongholds of clarity, and our spirits become lighthouses that shine brightly in the dark, all forged in the furnace of movement. Movement is the alchemy that turns adversity into opportunity, difficulty into strength, and pain into power, bringing us toward an inner state of fulfillment, wholeness, and balance.

The power of movement extends beyond the isolated domains of self-improvement and self-discovery and into the enormous web of unity, community, and human connection. We discover a sense of community, comradery, and solidarity in the group dance of movement, which binds us together in a common path of development, recovery, and progress. Movement is a language that cuts beyond words, boundaries, and differences to speak straight to the heart and create friendships, empathetic connections, and compassionate links that unite us and close the distance.

Fitness and contentment are not just things to strive for; rather, they are a way of life to adopt, an ideology to live by, and a legacy to pass on to next generations. Through the legacy of movement, we leave a blueprint for health, happiness, and harmony that cuts across time and place for our children, our communities, and the entire globe. Love for ourselves, for one another, and for the earth that supports us is the legacy of movement. It serves as a constant reminder of our interdependence, connectivity, and shared duty to take care of one another and ourselves.

Fitness and fulfilment are threads of light in the vast tapestry of life that lead us towards a state of wholeness, balance, and harmony that is in tune with the symphony of life. These threads illuminate the path of self-discovery, transformation, and empowerment. We rediscover our bodies as sacred vessels of power, resilience, and beauty that transport us toward our hopes and aspirations when we dance. Through this dance, we find joy, vitality, and purpose. Movement is our devoted companion and guide on this journey towards a life of health, happiness, and wholeness that feeds not just our bodies but also our hearts and souls. Fitness and fulfillment are not goals to be reached but rather a state of being.

Benefits of Regular Exercise

Frequent exercise is a holistic path towards cultivating a healthier, happier, and more meaningful life; it's not simply about working out hard at the gym or pounding the pavement. Engaging in regular physical activity has many advantages that go well beyond being more physically attractive. Exercise on a regular basis has transforming powers that improve every aspect of your life, from improving your mental health to raising your general quality of life.

Regular exercise has many significant benefits, one of which is its capacity to improve mood and reduce stress. Your body releases endorphins, sometimes known as the "feel-good" hormones, when you exercise. These neurotransmitters support you in overcoming emotions of stress, anxiety, and depression by acting as organic analgesics and mood enhancers. Frequent exercise has also been connected to lower levels of cortisol, the stress hormone, which improves your capacity to handle obstacles in life and have an optimistic attitude.

Furthermore, regular exercise can improve your mental clarity and cognitive efficiency dramatically. The synthesis of proteins called neurotrophic factors—which support the growth and development of new brain cells—is stimulated by physical activity. Thus, memory, focus, and general cognitive function are enhanced. Regular exercisers have been linked to improved mental clarity, improved problem-solving abilities, and a lower chance of cognitive deterioration as people age, according to research.

Regular exercise is essential for keeping a healthy weight and lowering the risk of chronic diseases, in addition to its positive effects on mental health. Physical activity is an essential part of weight management since it increases metabolism, burns calories, and builds muscle mass. You may lose extra weight and reduce your chance of getting diseases like diabetes, high blood pressure, and heart disease by adopting a balanced exercise routine.

Exercise on a regular basis is also a great way to strengthen your immune system and increase your general vigor. Increased circulation from physical activity makes it easier for immune cells to spread throughout the body and more successfully fight infections. Regular exercise improves your immune system, which lowers your vulnerability to infections and illnesses. This improves your quality of life and helps you stay active and resilient in the face of health issues.

Regular exercise also has the amazing benefit of enhancing the quality of sleep and encouraging peaceful sleeping. During the day, physical exercise promotes the release of melatonin, the hormone that induces sleep, and helps to balance your circadian cycle. Exercise has also been demonstrated to lessen insomnia symptoms and enhance overall sleep efficiency, enabling you to wake up feeling revitalized and prepared to take on the day.

Additionally, exercising on a daily basis is a powerful way to extend your life and improve your general quality of life. Engaging in physical activity not only helps to build stronger muscles and bones but also enhances cardiovascular health, lowers inflammation, and increases vitality. Making regular exercise a priority will help you age with more mobility, independence, and energy, allowing you to continue living an active and meaningful life well into your golden years.

This also promotes social support, a sense of belonging, and community—all of which are critical components of general wellbeing. Engaging in physical activity, whether on a sports team, in group fitness courses, or just working out with friends and family, offers a chance to connect with people, exchange stories, and build lasting relationships. These relationships with others not only improve your drive and responsibility but also foster a deep sense of community and belonging that profoundly improves your quality of life.

It has a profoundly positive impact on your body image, confidence, and sense of self. Being physically active enables you to value and honor your body for its potential, resiliency, and strength. Your sense of pride, empowerment, and success grows as you see your fitness levels increase and spread over all facets of your life, surpassing your outward look.

Exercise is also a great way to release pent-up emotions, tension, and negative energy. It is a potent stress reliever. Engaging in physical activity enables you to constructively channel your emotions, which improves your ability to handle and cope with the pressures of everyday life. Regular physical activity equips you to face life's obstacles with resiliency, grace, and composure, regardless of whether you like to work out hard to release steam or do mild workouts to decompress.

This helps you develop self-control, dedication, and tenacity, all of which have a positive impact on other aspects of your life. A regular fitness regimen requires commitment and consistency, which develops critical life skills like self-motivation, goal setting, and time management. You may cultivate a resilient mindset, a strong work ethic, and a growth-oriented attitude that will help you succeed and feel fulfilled in all facets of your life by practicing these traits through physical exercise.

To put it simply, the advantages of consistent exercise are as varied and life-changing as the people who partake in them. Regular exercise is essential to living a healthy, happy, and satisfying life since it improves your physical and mental health as well as builds community and connections. You can unleash a universe of possibilities, chances, and transformations that take you to new heights of health, happiness, and holistic well-being by making physical activity a priority and an essential part of your daily routine. Accept the power of consistent exercise, and allow it to lead you on a path of self-actualization, empowerment, and vigor that enhances each and every second of your life.

Types of Physical Activities

TAKING UP PHYSICAL activity can lead to a multitude of interesting and exciting opportunities to get your heart racing, your body moving, and your mood uplifted. The world of physical activities is a vivid tapestry of movement, rhythm, and expression that suits every taste, personality, and fitness level, ranging from intense workouts to calming mind-body techniques. Let's investigate the diverse range of physical activities that motivate, excite, and enliven people of all ages and backgrounds.

1. Cardiovascular Exercises: Providing heart health, endurance, and calorie burn, cardiovascular exercises are the foundation of physical fitness. Popular cardiovascular workouts that increase heart rate, strengthen cardiovascular function, and increase overall stamina include running, cycling, swimming, and dancing. These high-intensity exercises not only burn calories and improve physical fitness but also improve your mood, give you more energy, and give you a rush of excitement that keeps you moving forward.

2. Strength Training: Developing muscle growth, boosting bone density, and shaping a toned, muscular body all depend on strength training. Effective strength training techniques include weight lifting, resistance band activities, and bodyweight exercises like push-ups, squats, and planks. These techniques target certain muscle groups, improve functional strength, and support overall physical performance. You may increase metabolism, strengthen and resilient your body, and improve muscular tone by adding strength exercise to your program.

3. Flexibility and stretching: Increasing joint mobility, muscle elasticity, and general flexibility, flexibility exercises and stretching regimens are essential parts of a comprehensive fitness program. Stretching exercises, Pilates, and yoga all aid in improving alignment and posture, releasing muscle tension, and extending range of motion. These gentle yet effective exercises foster a profound sense of relaxation, mindfulness, and body awareness in addition to increasing physical flexibility and mobility.

4. High-intensity interval training, or HIIT, is a well-liked type of exercise that alternates short intervals of vigorous activity with slower-paced, lower-intensity sessions. Compared to conventional steady-state cardio, this high-octane training approach increases metabolism, burns fat, and enhances cardiovascular fitness in a shorter amount of time. Exercises that increase heart rate, test your body, and push you to new limits in strength and endurance include sprint intervals, burpees, and jump squats.

5. Dancing Fitness: If you want to get your body moving, groove to the music, and let your inner dancer loose, dancing fitness classes are an exciting and engaging option. Popular dance workouts like salsa dancing, hip-hop, ballet barre, and Zumba mix aerobic fitness with rhythmic movements. Through the power of dance, these dynamic and high-energy classes enhance self-expression, creativity, and joy in addition to enhancing coordination, balance, and agility.

6. Mind-Body Practices: By combining movement, breath work, and mindfulness, mind-body techniques like Tai Chi, Qigong, and meditation provide a comprehensive approach to physical well-being. These age-old techniques encourage inner harmony, balance, and serenity by promoting relaxation, stress reduction, and the mind-body connection. You may develop a focused and serene mindset, better your general mental and emotional

well-being, and improve your flexibility and posture by including mind-body exercises into your regimen.

7. Outdoor Activities: Engaging in outdoor activities is a terrific way to get your daily dosage of exercise and connect with nature. You may breathe fresh air, take in the breathtaking scenery, and connect with nature. Outdoor activities such as rock climbing, motorcycling, kayaking, and hiking are thrilling physical challenges that uplift your mood and stimulate your senses. Participating in outdoor activities cultivates a profound respect for the natural world, a spirit of adventure and exploration, and improves cardiovascular health and physical fitness.

8. Group Fitness Classes: If you're looking to get in shape and meet people who share your goals, group fitness classes provide an encouraging and supportive setting in which to work out and get sweaty. Group exercise classes, which range from Pilates and yoga to spinning and boot camp, offer a sense of accountability, community, and inspiration that energizes and motivates you. You may push yourself to the limit, take on new challenges, and celebrate your accomplishments with a community of like-minded fitness enthusiasts when you enroll in group fitness courses.

9. Combat Sports and Martial Arts: Martial arts styles like kickboxing, judo, taekwondo, and karate provide a special fusion of mental fortitude, physical training, and self-defense abilities. Practices in martial arts and combat sports develop attention, perseverance, and self-confidence in addition to strengthening one's strength, agility, and coordination. These stimulating and energizing practices test your body and mind, foster self-control and self-respect, and enable you to discover your inner warrior.

10. Water-Based Activities: Swimming, aqua aerobics, and water polo are a few examples of water-based sports that offer a cool, low-impact method to keep active, build muscle, and enhance cardiovascular health. Engaging in water activities provides resistance and buoyancy that improve cardiovascular endurance, joint flexibility, muscular tone, and joint stress while lowering the chance of injury. Water-based activities provide an exciting and refreshing way to keep active and have fun, whether you're gliding through the water or splashing in the pool.

11. Adventure Sports and Recreation: Activities that test your limitations, push your body, and embrace the spirit of adventure, such as surfing, rock

climbing, skiing, and snowboarding, provide an exhilarating and thrilling experience. These intense activities develop bravery, resiliency, and daring in addition to improving physical fitness, coordination, and agility. Adventure sports provide you with the opportunity to step outside of your comfort zone, face your anxieties, and feel the rush of pushing your body and mind to new and exciting limits.

12. Recreational Sports: Playing team sports like volleyball, basketball, tennis, and soccer can help you keep active, improve your abilities, and have fun in a competitive and social setting. Recreational sports participation develops teamwork, sportsmanship, and mutual support in addition to cardiovascular fitness, agility, and coordination. Recreational sports, whether you're serving on the tennis court or dribbling on the basketball court, provide an exciting and engaging opportunity to have fun, keep in shape, and create lifelong friendships.

You can discover the ideal balance of exercise that suits your tastes, objectives, and interests by incorporating a variety of physical activities into your routine. Whether you're looking for a high-intensity challenge, a calming stretch, or an adrenaline rush, the world of physical sports beckons with limitless opportunities for personal development. Through the art of physical activity, nurture your body, mind, and soul as you embrace the joy of movement and the power of your body. This is the beginning of a journey toward holistic well-being.

Integrating Exercise into Daily Life

Starting the process of incorporating exercise into your daily routine is like starting to weave a fabric of health, energy, and fortitude that enhances every strand of your life. It may seem impossible to find time for physical activity in the middle of the chaos of everyday life in this fast-paced world where time is a valuable resource and schedules are full. But you can easily incorporate movement, energy, and vitality into your daily routine with a dash of imagination, a sprinkle of intention, and a dollop of commitment. This will turn exercise from a chore into a delightful, energizing habit that feeds your body, mind, and soul.

Imagine starting your day with a revitalizing yoga flow that awakens your body, concentrates your mind, and creates a positive vibe for the day ahead as you wake up to the soft touch of the morning sun, rather than going for your phone. Your body moves fluidly and your breath flows rhythmically, combining to create a symphony of movement and mindfulness that grounds you in the present and gives you a sense of peace and energy. You feel your muscles waking up, stress dissipating, and energy coursing through your veins with each stretch, twist, and bend, readying you to face the day with elegance and power.

You take advantage of every chance to smuggle in little bursts of exercise that become a seamless part of your everyday schedule while juggling the demands of job, family, and obligations. To keep your body moving, posture straight, and energy flowing during virtual meetings, try doing chair yoga postures, desk stretches, or mini squats. You choose to take a fast walk around the block, a quick dance to your favorite music, or a series of bodyweight exercises that improve your mood, revitalize your body, and clear your head during your lunch break.

As night falls like a gentle curtain, you take comfort in the steady beat of your nighttime jog, bike ride, or dancing class, which is a ritual that nourishes your spirit, releases pent energy, and honors your body's tenacity and fortitude. You are grounded in the present, stress is released, and your spirit is rejuvenated by the symphony of movement, passion, and freedom created by the pavement beneath your feet, the wind in your hair, and the rhythmic pulse of your heart. You advance with every step, pedal, or leap, bringing with you a wave of empowerment, clarity, and joy and ushering out the cares and troubles of the day.

Weekends unfold like a blank canvas, full of opportunity to discover new places, increase your level of physical fitness, and engage in joyful, movement-filled leisure activities. Whether you're taking a hike in the embrace of nature, paddle boarding across shimmering waters, or doing outdoor yoga under the sun, weekends turn into a playground of movement, discovery, and renewal that reenergizes your body, refreshes your soul, and strengthens your bond with the natural world.

Including exercise in your daily routine takes you beyond the domain of physical health and into a holistic practice that supports the harmonic balance of your body, mind, and soul. It is a deliberate decision to give self-care, wellbeing, and vitality top priority in a world full of distractions and expectations rather than just something to cross off your to-do list. Your everyday routine becomes a seamless tapestry of health, joy, and empowerment when you weave movement into it. This uplifts, maintains, and moves you closer to a life of holistic well-being and fulfillment.

The kitchen, the center of the house, is where you may turn menial chores like cleaning and cooking into chances for exercise and meditation. You move in place of being motionless by swaying to your favorite music, squatting and lunging while waiting for the water to boil, or shimmying while chopping vegetables. You burn calories, enhance coordination, tone muscles, and infuse ordinary activities with a feeling of humor and delight when you dance and groove in the kitchen. This enlivens your spirit and feeds your body.

Your workout regimen is fueled by a sense of camaraderie, support, and shared purpose that comes from the power of community and social connections, which in turn increases your motivation, commitment, and joy. Joining a fitness class with friends, going on a hike with like-minded people, or taking part in an online workout challenge with friends all build a web of support, inspiration, and accountability that not only elevates your fitness journey but also fosters a sense of belonging and connection.

When it comes to incorporating exercise into your daily routine, technology can be a great ally. There are a tonne of fitness applications, wearable technology, and internet resources available that can help you measure your progress, give you advice, and stay educated and inspired. Technology enables you to personalize your fitness journey, set goals, track performance, and connect with a global community of fitness enthusiasts, experts, and mentors who inspire, motivate, and guide you towards your health and wellness aspirations. These resources range from interactive challenges and community forums to personalized workout plans and virtual training sessions.

When it comes to creative expression, movement serves as a blank canvas for change, self-expression, and self-discovery that reaches beyond the bounds of traditional exercise and into the domain of artistry and imagination. With movement that speaks to your soul, fires your passion, and liberates your spirit, you can express your inner rhythms and emotions while dancing as if no one else is around. Flow like a river. Whether you use your body to paint in a dance performance, shape your body through yoga poses, or practice martial arts as a way to express yourself, movement becomes a vehicle for self-expression, personal development, and self-discovery that goes beyond physical limitations and opens up your limitless potential.

Movement becomes a sacred practice of presence, awareness, and inner connection when it is combined with the art of mindfulness and meditation. This strengthens your connection to your body, breath, and spirit. You can develop a strong sense of connection to the present now, awaken your senses, and listen into the gentle whispers of your body's wisdom and intuition by engaging in mindful movement. Whether you're moving mindfully to practice Tai Chi in the morning light, stroll in quiet reflection, or flow through a gentle yoga sequence, these activities open doors to inner peace, clarity, and self-awareness that feed your spirit, calm your mind, and bring you into harmony with the graceful unfolding rhythm of life.

By engaging in mindful activities that nourish your body, calm your mind, and uplift your soul, you acknowledge your body's need for repair, recovery, and renewal when the day comes to an end and you sink into the embrace of rest and rebirth. You construct a sanctuary of self-care, peace, and tranquility that guides you into a state of profound relaxation, rejuvenation, and rebirth. This sanctuary can include anything from gentle stretches and deep breathing exercises to guided relaxation techniques and calming bedtime yoga sequences. You develop an inner feeling of balance, harmony, and serenity with every breath, every stretch, and every quiet moment. This inner peace empowers you to greet each day with grace, resiliency, and vigor.

Integrating exercise becomes a thread in the fabric of daily life, weaving together moments of movement, mindfulness, creativity, and connection to create a colorful and seamless mosaic of happiness, holistic health, and well-being. Exercise becomes more than just a chore or a habit when you include deliberate movement, mindful awareness, and joyous expression into every part of your day. This celebrates the body's innate power, resilience, and beauty. You honor your body as a temple of vitality, a vessel of inspiration, and a canvas of opportunity with each stride, breath, and movement. It is an invitation to dance, play, explore, and express the limitless potential and beauty that are inside of you.

So, dear seeker of well-being, learn to enjoy movement and turn it into a profound act of self-love and self-care by embracing the art of incorporating exercise into your everyday life with a spirit of inquiry, creativity, and devotion. The power of embodying vitality, presence, and resilience in every aspect of your life should be demonstrated by every moment, breath, and movement. Fill each day with the radiant energy, vibrant vitality, and limitless joy that come from living in harmony with the rhythm of movement, the melody of mindfulness, and the dance of holistic health and well-being.

CHAPTER 6
Investing in Longevity

In this day and age of swift progress and unceasing change, we all strive for longevity—the skill of living fully and healthily for a prolonged amount of time. Investing in longevity requires more than just extending our lives; it also entails promoting our mental, emotional, and physical health via sustainable activities that open doors to a better future for current and future generations. Prioritizing longevity-supporting sustainable behaviors becomes not only a choice, but also essential for thriving in the face of changing challenges and complexities in a world where life seems to be moving at an ever-increasing pace.

The idea of holistic health, which includes the mental, emotional, spiritual, and physical aspects of our well-being, is fundamental to investing in longevity. In addition to taking care of our bodies with a healthy diet, consistent exercise, and enough sleep, sustainable habits that lengthen life also require taking care of our minds with emotional stability, mental stimulation, and stress reduction methods. By addressing our health and well-being holistically, we build a solid foundation for longevity and give ourselves the ability to face life's curveballs with grace, vigor, and resilience.

When it comes to nutrition, investing in longevity means developing a conscious and sustainable relationship with food—a relationship that nourishes our bodies, upholds our health, and preserves the environment. Adopting a plant-based diet full of fruits, vegetables, whole grains, and legumes not only minimizes our environmental footprint but also supplies vital nutrients and antioxidants for optimum health. Selecting seasonal, organic, and locally grown food supports sustainable agricultural methods that safeguard biodiversity, conserve natural resources, and lessen the consequences of climate change—all of which are beneficial to the environment and human health.

Another important component of investing in longevity is physical activity. Exercise improves our mood, cognitive function, and general quality of life in addition to strengthening our muscles, bones, and cardiovascular system. Adding movement to our daily lives by engaging in enjoyable activities like dancing, walking, cycling, or swimming improves our mental and emotional health as well as our physical fitness and fosters social interaction. By incorporating regular, pleasant exercise into our lives, we improve our quality of life and promote longevity by developing a mindset of vitality, energy, and resilience.

As they support us in developing inner calm, emotional balance, and resilience in the face of life's obstacles and uncertainties, mindfulness and stress management techniques are essential for investing in longevity. Deep breathing techniques, yoga, and mindfulness meditation teach us to create an inner peace, presence, and awareness that improves our mental health, lowers stress levels, and promotes longevity. We give ourselves the tools to handle life's ups and downs with resilience, grace, and composure by cultivating healthy coping strategies for stress and embracing a positive attitude on life.

Investing in longevity requires social ties and community involvement because they provide us a sense of purpose, support, and belonging that improves our quality of life and nurtures our emotional health. In addition to lowering feelings of loneliness and isolation, developing strong social networks, cultivating meaningful connections, and getting involved in community activities significantly increase mental health, emotional resilience, and lifespan. We build a sense of community, support, and purpose by making meaningful connections with others and investing in our social networks. This enhances our lives and makes us more resilient to life's setbacks.

Investing in longevity and environmental sustainability are inextricably linked since the state of the earth has a direct impact on our health and happiness. By incorporating eco-friendly habits into our daily lives—like cutting back on trash, using less energy, and promoting the use of renewable resources—we help create a healthier ecosystem that benefits not just present and future generations, but also ourselves. We leave a legacy of environmental stewardship, health, and well-being that promotes longevity and guarantees a healthy future for everybody when we make deliberate decisions that put sustainability first.

Advancements in healthcare and innovative technologies are essential for investing in longevity because they give us access to individualized wellness programs, preventive care, and state-of-the-art therapies that improve our lifespan and overall health. Technology gives us the ability to take charge of our health, make educated decisions, and access healthcare services that promote longevity—from wearables that measure our health data to telemedicine services that offer virtual consultations. We are ushering in a new era of personalized and preventive care that enables us to live longer, healthier, and more satisfying lives by embracing technological breakthroughs and utilizing digital tools to support our health and well-being.

Investing in longevity requires us to engage in lifelong learning and personal growth, which broadens our horizons, ignites our passions, and stimulates our minds in ways that improve our emotional health, sense of purpose, and cognitive performance. Through participating in lifelong learning, pursuing artistic efforts, and discovering novel hobbies, we provide nourishment to our minds, stimulate our intellect, and foster a sense of wonder and curiosity that enhances our lives and promotes longevity. A growth mindset and an embrace of lifelong learning allow us to be more receptive to opportunities, insights, and experiences that enhance our resilience, well-being, and personal development.

Making an investment in longevity through sustainable behaviors is a path of self-awareness, development, and empowerment that supports our health, vitality, and well-being in ways that go beyond age and time constraints. Through adopting a comprehensive perspective on our health and overall well-being, giving importance to long-term sustainable practices, and utilizing cutting-edge innovations and technologies to improve our standard of living, we chart a course for a more prosperous, happier, and healthier future for ourselves and future generations. By making an investment in longevity, we contribute to a sustainable, dynamic, and resilient future where longevity, health, and well-being are valued as the priceless assets that they are. We are also investing in ourselves.

Building Healthy Habits for Life

Developing wholesome routines that will sustain us throughout time and provide us with nourishment on a daily basis is one of the most important journeys we take as we traverse the enormous terrain of life. Developing lifelong healthy habits is a dynamic and evolving process that calls for attention, dedication, and a thorough understanding of our unique needs and values. It is not just about following a fixed routine or checklist. It is about developing long-lasting habits that enhance our mental, emotional, and physical health and enable us to flourish and fully experience life.

The power of intention sits at the heart of creating lifelong healthy habits. Making decisions that support our health and well-being is made easier when we have clear intentions, which enables us to match our actions with our values and objectives. Whether it's setting aside time for self-care, making a daily commitment to exercise, or giving nutritious meals top priority, intention acts as a compass to guide us toward behaviors that support our body, mind, and soul. By grounding our routines in intention, we develop a feeling of direction and purpose that strengthens our resolve to maintain long-term health and vitality.

The foundation of creating long-lasting, healthy behaviors is consistency. The secret to bringing about long-lasting change and incorporating new habits into our daily lives is consistent action, no matter how tiny. Consistency strengthens the neural networks that support our behaviors, which makes them more natural and effortless over time. Examples of these neural pathways include walking every day, drinking enough water, and engaging in mindfulness practices. Consistently putting ourselves first helps us to develop discipline, resilience, and self-trust—all of which are necessary for long-term well-being and lasting transformation. It also reinforces our behaviors.

Developing adaptable habits is essential to creating lifelong healthy habits. Because life is dynamic and constantly changing, our habits must be adaptable enough to change along with us. To be flexible is to be open to modifying our routines in response to evolving demands, situations, and priorities. It's about coming up with innovative solutions, adjusting to difficulties, and gracefully and resiliently accepting life's ups and downs. By developing habits that are flexible, we enable ourselves to handle life's curveballs with dexterity, imagination, and a sense of wonder that keeps our routines new, applicable, and long-lasting.

A key component of developing wholesome routines that are consistent with our true selves is self-awareness. By reflecting on our motives, values, and routines, we can better understand what genuinely energizes and nourishes us. It involves becoming attuned to our inner wisdom, emotions, and bodily cues in order to recognize the patterns that promote our happiness and overall well-being. By developing self-awareness, we gain a thorough grasp of who we are and what we need, which enables us to make decisions that are consistent with our morals and promote our general well-being.

A useful strategy for creating wholesome routines that support balance and well-being in our lives is mindfulness. Making deliberate decisions that promote our health and vitality is made possible when we are judgment-free and fully present in the moment. It involves developing an awareness of our thoughts, feelings, and behaviors while we go about our regular lives. This strengthens our sense of self and connectedness to the outside world. We can develop a sense of present, attentiveness, and gratitude via the regular practice of mindfulness, which enhances our everyday experiences and fosters overall well-being.

A vital part of creating lifelong healthy habits is self-care. Maintaining our general health and vitality requires taking care of our physical, mental, and emotional needs. Self-care can take many different forms, such as making time for rest and relaxation or doing things that make us happy and fulfilled. Making self-care a priority in our everyday lives helps us feel more balanced and resilient, refill our energy, and lower our stress levels—all of which contribute to our long-term health and well-being. In order to create lifelong healthy habits, self-care is not a luxury but rather a need.

Building long-lasting healthy behaviors is greatly aided by social and community support. Having a supporting network around us, whether it be virtual or real-world, can help us stay motivated, accountable, and inspired while we pursue our health goals. Our drive and dedication to our habits are fueled by the sense of connection, camaraderie, and shared purpose that arises from sharing our objectives, struggles, and achievements with others. In addition to fortifying our routines, we also promote a feeling of community, support, and mutual development that ultimately improves our resilience and general well-being.

Developing healthy habits that adapt to our changing circumstances throughout time requires a lifetime of learning and development. Our minds are profoundly nourished, our horizons are expanded, and our well-being is profoundly enhanced when we pursue ongoing education, take up new hobbies, and look for personal growth chances. We may remain receptive to fresh opportunities, realizations, and experiences that enhance our lives and enable us to change and develop gracefully and resiliently by embracing a growth mindset and lifelong learning. Developing a curious, open-hearted outlook on life that promotes our growth and well-being in all facets of our being is also an important part of lifelong learning.

When it comes to creating engaging, gratifying, and durable healthy habits, innovation and creativity are crucial components. We may keep ahead of the curve, adjust to changing conditions, and discover new avenues for our health journey by embracing new concepts, tools, and methods related to health and well-being. Innovation and creativity give our routines a breath of fresh air, excitement, and vitality that inspires and motivates us to pursue a healthy lifestyle for life. Examples of this include incorporating mindfulness practices into our daily routine, trying out new workout routines, and experimenting with plant-based recipes.

Essentially, developing lifelong healthy habits is an exciting and empowering process that gives us the ability to create routines that will ultimately promote our fulfillment, energy, and overall well-being. We build a foundation for a healthy and vibrant existence that connects with our actual selves by establishing habits that are anchored in intention, consistency, adaptability, self-awareness, mindfulness, self-care, community support, growth, innovation, and creativity. We invest in our current well-being when we embrace the adventure of developing lifelong healthy habits, but we also create the foundation for a future full of energy, resiliency, and joy—a future in which fulfillment, happiness, and health are our constant companions on the amazing trip that is life.

Preventive Healthcare Measures

The unsung heroes of our health are preventive healthcare practices; they are the silent protectors who toil diligently in the background to preserve our energy and health. These precautions serve as beacons of knowledge and foresight, pointing the way towards a path of longevity and wellbeing in a world where the rush of daily life can occasionally overshadow the significance of prevention. See them as the quiet conductors of our health symphony, guiding us through the ages in a tuneful melody that shields us from the discordant notes of disease and illness.

The power of information and awareness is at the core of preventative healthcare practices. It's been stated that prevention is preferable to treatment, and knowledge really is the key to opening the door to a healthier future. We empower ourselves to take proactive measures to maintain our well-being by educating ourselves about the risk factors, warning signals, and preventative tactics for common health disorders. Knowledge is more than simply power; it is the compass that points us in the direction of wise decisions and actions that stop illness before it starts.

Routine health examinations and screenings are among the core components of preventative healthcare. Regular evaluations play the role of health detectives, identifying possible health concerns before they become more serious ones. These screenings, which range from mammograms to colonoscopies, from blood pressure checks to cholesterol tests, offer important insights into our health state and assist in identifying diseases early on when they are most treatable. We invest in our long-term health and well-being by prioritizing health screenings in our routine healthcare, giving ourselves the gift of early diagnosis and prevention.

Another essential component of preventative healthcare that has enormous influence over our health outcomes is nutrition. Food serves as more than simply bodily sustenance; it is also a kind of medication that can either help or hurt us. One of the best preventive actions we can take to safeguard our health is to adopt a diet that is well-balanced and nutrient-rich, with an emphasis on fruits, vegetables, whole grains, lean meats, and healthy fats. By feeding our bodies healthful foods and making thoughtful dietary decisions, we strengthen our immune system, nourish our essential organs, and lower our chance of developing chronic illnesses like obesity, diabetes, and heart disease.

Engaging in physical activity can serve as a powerful preventive measure with numerous advantages for our overall health and welfare. Frequent exercise improves mood, improves cognitive function, lowers the risk of many health disorders, and strengthens our muscles and cardiovascular system. There are a plethora of options for being active and incorporating movement into our daily lives, ranging from vigorous walks to yoga sessions, strength training to dancing courses. We invest in our physical, mental, and emotional well-being when we prioritize physical activity as a preventive approach. The benefits include a more resilient and lively body and mind.

In our fast-paced society, stress management is an essential part of preventative healthcare that is sometimes disregarded. A variety of health issues, including immunological malfunction and heart disease, have been related to chronic stress, thus learning healthy coping mechanisms to reduce stress and encourage relaxation is crucial. Deep breathing exercises, yoga, and other mindfulness activities can help us better regulate our stress levels, build resilience, and improve our general sense of well-being. We may build a barrier against the negative effects of stress and foster inner peace and harmony by implementing stress management practices into our daily lives.

Sleep is an effective preventive strategy that is frequently disregarded yet is crucial to preserving our health and energy. Immune system performance, cell repair, cognitive function, and general wellbeing all depend on getting enough good sleep. However, in today's society, sleep is frequently forgone in favor of entertainment or work. Our bodies heal naturally, and we strengthen our immune system against illness and disease by prioritizing restful sleep and forming healthy sleep habits, such as keeping a regular sleep schedule, building a calming bedtime routine, and optimizing our sleep surroundings.

A key component of preventive healthcare, which has transformed the field of public health and illness prevention, is vaccination. Vaccines have greatly decreased the global burden of infectious illnesses and have been instrumental in the eradication of terrible diseases like polio and smallpox. By ensuring that we and our loved ones receive the prescribed vaccines on time, we not only maintain our personal health but also build community immunity, protecting the weak and halting the spread of infectious diseases.

Changes in lifestyle, such giving up drinking, stopping smoking, and keeping a healthy weight, are important preventive steps that can significantly improve our health results. In the world, smoking is one of the biggest preventable causes of mortality, and drinking too much alcohol is associated with a host of health issues, including cancer and liver disease. By adopting better lifestyle decisions and kicking bad habits, we give ourselves the ability to take charge of our health and lower our chance of developing chronic illnesses, which can have a major negative influence on our quality of life.

Oral hygiene routines and routine dental exams are essential preventive measures that improve our general health in addition to safeguarding our teeth and gums. The correlation between insufficient dental hygiene and systemic ailments such as diabetes, heart disease, and respiratory infections emphasizes the significance of upholding proper oral hygiene practices. Regular dental checkups, good brushing and flossing habits, and eating a diet high in dental-friendly foods help maintain our oral health and lower our chance of developing dental issues that could negatively affect our general health and quality of life.

Building a solid support system and getting mental health treatment when necessary are crucial preventive steps that enhance resilience and emotional well-being. It has been demonstrated that having social ties improves mental health, lowers stress, and enhances general quality of life. We can avoid feelings of loneliness and isolation by fostering ties with friends, family, and neighbors. These interactions provide as a safety net of support for us while we negotiate life's obstacles. Additionally, sustaining emotional well-being and delaying the onset of more serious mental health diseases can be achieved by obtaining professional assistance when dealing with mental health issues like anxiety, sadness, or trauma.

Preventive healthcare practices are essentially the cornerstones upon which we construct a life full of health, energy, and wellbeing. Through embracing information, screenings, diet, exercise, stress reduction, sleep hygiene, immunizations, lifestyle adjustments, dental care, and emotional support, we build a holistic barrier that protects our health for the duration of our lives. These preventative efforts are not only isolated acts; rather, they are threads that collectively create a tapestry of longevity, resilience, and wellbeing that honors the role that prevention plays in ensuring that each of us has a healthier and more promising future.

Planning for Long-Term Wellness

Long-term wellbeing is a journey to be embraced, one that involves deliberate decisions and activities and is not a destination to be reached but rather a voyage of self-discovery and empowerment. Imagine it as a vivid mosaic, where every tiny choice and habit we make contributes a vibrant tile to the overall picture of our wellbeing. Long-term wellness planning is similar to caring for a garden: with careful preparation, tender care, and persistent work, a plentiful crop of health and vitality is produced.

The art of mindful living—a purposeful and aware approach to making everyday decisions that prioritize our physical, mental, and emotional well-being—lays the foundation for long-term wellness planning. It's about developing a close relationship with ourselves, paying attention to the subtle messages from our body and spirit, and respecting our inner knowledge. We can steer toward enduring health and vitality that is based on self-awareness and self-care by paying attention to our needs and desires.

A holistic state of balance and harmony that includes our physical, mental, and emotional aspects is what is meant to be understood as health, not merely the absence of disease. When we set out to prepare for long-term wellness, we make a commitment to nourishing every part of ourselves and building a strong base for a happy and healthy life. Self-care, good habits, and an optimistic outlook serve as the cornerstones of this foundation, which serves as a roadmap for long-term optimal health and wellbeing.

Setting attainable objectives that are consistent with our priorities, aspirations, and beliefs is essential to long-term wellness planning. By serving as compass points, these objectives help us focus our efforts and energies on the idea of a happier and healthier future. Whether the objective is to reduce stress, adopt a balanced diet, exercise regularly, improve sleep habits, or foster social relationships, having a wellness roadmap that is both clear and actionable can help us succeed in our endeavors.

A continuous and steadfast dedication to our health and well-being goals, especially in the face of obstacles and disappointments, is the cornerstone of long-term wellness planning. Little, enduring habits that are practiced every day add up to produce big, long-lasting change over time. We build resilience, discipline, and tenacity by being consistent in our wellness routines; this paves the way for long-lasting health and vitality.

Another essential component of long-term wellness planning is flexibility, or the ability to modify our objectives and tactics in response to evolving conditions and demands. Since life is a dynamic and always changing journey, our health strategies need to be adaptable and sensitive to the ups and downs of our experiences. We may develop a resilient and resourceful attitude that equips us to handle life's curveballs with grace and adaptation by embracing flexibility.

Long-term wellness planning cannot include self-care—the dedication to taking care of our physical, mental, and emotional needs—as a negotiable element. Self-care is an essential investment in our health and well-being that keeps us resilient and restores our energy. It is not selfish. Self-care is the gasoline that drives our path to long-lasting wellness, from setting aside time for rest and renewal to partaking in joyful and fulfilling activities.

A major component of long-term wellness planning is mindful eating, which is a deliberate and mindful approach to providing our bodies with healthful, nourishing foods. By being aware of our hunger signals, enjoying every meal, and selecting foods that fill us up, we may develop a positive connection with food and improve our general health. The goal of mindful eating is to develop an awareness and appreciation for the nutritious gifts of nature that support our health and vitality, rather than to restrict or deprive ourselves.

Another component of long-term wellness planning is physical activity, which is the dedication to moving our bodies frequently and partaking in exercises that increase strength, agility, and endurance. Exercise honors the marvelous gift of our bodies and celebrates the joy of movement, not only the goal of gaining muscle or burning calories. The secret to maintaining a lifetime commitment to physical well-being is to identify activities that bring us joy and vitality, whether that means taking brisk walks in the outdoors or intense workouts at the gym.

Understanding the interdependence of mind, body, and spirit in determining our health and happiness makes mental and emotional wellness equally significant components of long-term wellness planning. To lay a solid basis for mental and emotional well-being, one must practice gratitude and self-compassion, foster good relationships, cultivate a positive outlook, and ask for help when necessary. We build a feeling of balance and harmony that gets us through life's challenges and strengthen ourselves against life's storms by cultivating resilience, emotional intelligence, and inner serenity.

In long-term wellness planning, social relationships are a potent source of support and enrichment—a constant reminder of our humanity and connectivity. Meaningful relationships with friends, family, coworkers, and neighbors not only add love, humor, and a sense of belonging to our lives, but they also act as a support system and source of encouragement when we need it most. Building social networks and a feeling of community improves our general wellbeing and increases our capacity for emotional resilience. These actions set the stage for a life full of joy, meaning, and connection.

Planning for long-term wellness is essentially a voyage of self-awareness, empowerment, and metamorphosis that is facilitated by deliberate decision-making, thoughtful living, and a dedication to wellbeing and self-care. We build a strong foundation for persistent health and vitality across the lifespan by establishing clear goals, practicing consistency, embracing flexibility, and nurturing every facet of our being. Long-term wellness planning is a way of life to embrace rather than a goal to be reached; it is a route that points us in the direction of a future full of fulfillment, health, and pleasure.

Some of these has been stated earlier in this book.

CONCLUSION

As we draw the curtains on the profound exploration of the mantra "Wellness Over Fortune: Investing in Health Pays the Best Dividends," it becomes unequivocally clear that this philosophy transcends mere financial gain—it embodies a profound paradigm shift in our understanding of wealth, success, and fulfillment. In delving deep into the woven tapestry of human existence, we uncover a timeless truth that resonates with the core of our being—a truth that beckons us to prioritize our well-being above all else.

The essence of this mantra lies in its call to action—an invitation to embark on a journey of self-discovery, self-care, and self-nourishment. It challenges us to redefine prosperity not as the accumulation of external riches, but as the cultivation of internal riches—vibrant health, inner peace, and holistic well-being. In a world where the pursuit of monetary wealth often takes precedence, the wisdom encapsulated in "Wellness Over Fortune" serves as a guiding light, illuminating a path to true abundance and fulfillment.

Investing in health is not simply a matter of ticking boxes on a wellness checklist—it is a profound act of self-love, self-respect, and self-preservation. It is a declaration of our intrinsic worth, a recognition of the sacred vessel that houses our essence. When we prioritize our health, we sow the seeds for a future brimming with vitality, resilience, and joy. The dividends of such investments go beyond the quantifiable—they manifest in the form of enhanced quality of life, deeper connections, and a sense of purpose that transcends material wealth.

By choosing wellness over fortune, we defy conventional notions of success and prosperity. We acknowledge that true wealth is not measured in bank balances or possessions, but in the moments of grace, gratitude, and growth that enrich our lives. The dividends of investing in health are manifold—they ripple through every aspect of our being, nourishing our body, mind, and spirit with abundance and vitality. In embracing this philosophy, we lay the foundation for a life lived in alignment with our truest values and aspirations.

The act of investing in health is a testament to our commitment to personal growth, evolution, and self-empowerment. It requires us to make conscious choices that honor our well-being, nurture our potential, and cultivate a state of wholeness that transcends external circumstances. When we prioritize wellness, we gift ourselves with the greatest treasure of all—a life lived with intention, purpose, and authenticity.

In a world that often equates success with external accolades and material possessions, the mantra "Wellness Over Fortune" stands as a radical reimagining of prosperity—a reminder that true wealth resides within us, waiting to be unlocked and embraced. When we choose to invest in our health, we invest in a future defined by vitality, joy, and resilience. The fruits of such investments flow outward, influencing the lives of others around us and producing a ripple effect of well-being and positivity.

As we contemplate on the enormous ramifications of valuing wellness above fortune, we are reminded of the intrinsic interconnectivity of all elements of our existence. Health is not only the absence of illness—it is a condition of fullness that comprises physical energy, mental clarity, emotional balance, and spiritual harmony. When we invest in our health, we invest in a future where each facet of our being is nourished, nurtured, and appreciated.

It conveys a profound truth that connects with the heart of our being. It encourages us to reevaluate our priorities, reassess our values, and realign our actions with our deepest goals. By choosing to prioritize our well-being, we embark on a transforming path of self-discovery and self-empowerment—a journey that promises a future rich with energy, abundance, and joy. As we embrace this belief, we step into our full power as conscious creators of our destiny, designing a life of meaning, purpose, and fulfillment.

| Page

Don't miss out!

Visit the website below and you can sign up to receive emails whenever MORGAN HARTWELL publishes a new book. There's no charge and no obligation.

https://books2read.com/r/B-A-WTHVC-BPMIF

BOOKS2READ

Connecting independent readers to independent writers.

Did you love *Wellness Over Fortune: Investing in Heath Pays The Best Dividends*? Then you should read *Make a Fucking Dollar Today : Your Path to Enacting Financial Prosperity*[1] by Paul R. Frederick!

Are you tired of living paycheck to paycheck, struggling to make ends meet, and feeling like financial freedom is nothing more than a distant dream? It's time to take control of your financial destiny and embark on a journey that will transform your relationship with money, elevate your income potential, and pave the way for everlasting prosperity. Welcome to "Make a Fucking Dollar Today - Your Path to Enacting Financial Prosperity," a groundbreaking guide that will revolutionize the way you perceive wealth, empower you to unleash your earning potential, and equip you with the tools to create a life of abundance and financial security.

Attention: Have you ever felt stuck in a cycle of financial mediocrity, watching as others around you seem to effortlessly climb the ladder of success while you remain stagnant? It's time to break free from the chains of financial

---

1. https://books2read.com/u/mgD6X6

2. https://books2read.com/u/mgD6X6

limitations and embark on a path that will lead you towards financial independence, wealth accumulation, and the lifestyle you've always desired. "Make a Fucking Dollar Today" is not just a book; it's a manifesto for those who refuse to settle for mediocrity and are ready to embrace their potential for greatness.

Imagine a life where your bank account is brimming with wealth, your investments are flourishing, and you have the freedom to live on your own terms without worrying about financial constraints. This is the reality that awaits you when you commit to enacting financial prosperity through the transformative principles outlined in this book.

It's time to stop waiting for financial success to come knocking at your door and start taking decisive action towards building the life you deserve. "Make a Fucking Dollar Today" provides you with a roadmap to financial prosperity, guiding you through the steps to transform your mindset, supercharge your income, budget effectively, invest wisely, and arm yourself with the financial knowledge necessary to thrive in any economic landscape. The time for action is now, and the path to enacting financial prosperity is laid out before you, waiting for you to seize it with determination and purpose.

As you delve into the pages of "Make a Fucking Dollar Today," you will discover:

- The power of mindset and motivation in reshaping your relationship with money and unleashing your full potential for wealth creation.
- Proven strategies for generating multiple streams of income, whether through side hustles, entrepreneurship, investments, or passive income sources.
- Budgeting techniques that will help you take control of your finances, optimize your spending, and pave the way for lasting financial stability.
- Investment insights and wealth-building principles that will enable you to grow your assets, secure your financial future, and achieve financial independence.
- The importance of continuous financial education and literacy in empowering you to make informed decisions, navigate financial challenges, and seize opportunities for growth and prosperity.

In a world where financial uncertainties abound and the quest for financial freedom seems daunting, "Make a Fucking Dollar Today" serves as a beacon of hope, a roadmap to prosperity, and a guide to unlocking your full potential for wealth and success. It's time to stop settling for less, start creating the life you deserve, and make fucking dollars today that will pave the way to a future filled with abundance, security, and prosperity. Embrace the journey, seize the opportunities, and let "Make a Fucking Dollar Today" be the catalyst that propels you towards financial greatness. Your path to enacting financial prosperity starts now.

Also by MORGAN HARTWELL

Wellness Over Fortune: Investing in Heath Pays The Best Dividends